PENGUIN BOOKS

ON ANARCHISM

Noam Chomsky is the author of numerous bestselling political books, including *Hegemony or Survival, Failed States, Interventions, What We Say Goes, Hopes and Prospects, Occupy* and *Power Systems*, all of which are published by Hamish Hamilton/Penguin. He is a professor in the Department of Linguistics and Philosophy at MIT, and is widely credited with having revolutionized modern linguistics.

Nathan Schneider is the author of *Thank You, Anarchy: Notes from the Occupy Apocalypse* and *God in Proof: The Story of a Search from the Ancients to the Internet*. He also edits the online publications *Waging Nonviolence* and *Killing the Buddha*. He lives in Brooklyn, New York.

On Anarchism

Noam Chomsky

PENGUIN BOOKS

PENGUIN BOOKS

Published by the Penguin Group
Penguin Books Ltd, 80 Strand, London WC2R 0RL, England
Penguin Group (USA) Inc., 375 Hudson Street, New York, New York 10014, USA
Penguin Group (Canada), 90 Eglinton Avenue East, Suite 700, Toronto, Ontario, Canada M4P 2Y3
(a division of Pearson Penguin Canada Inc.)
Penguin Ireland, 25 St Stephen's Green, Dublin 2, Ireland (a division of Penguin Books Ltd)
Penguin Group (Australia), 707 Collins Street, Melbourne, Victoria 3008, Australia
(a division of Pearson Australia Group Pty Ltd)
Penguin Books India Pvt Ltd, 11 Community Centre, Panchsheel Park, New Delhi – 110 017, India
Penguin Group (NZ), 67 Apollo Drive, Rosedale, Auckland 0632, New Zealand
(a division of Pearson New Zealand Ltd)
Penguin Books (South Africa) (Pty) Ltd, Block D, Rosebank Office Park,
181 Jan Smuts Avenue, Parktown North, Gauteng 2193, South Africa

Penguin Books Ltd, Registered Offices: 80 Strand, London WC2R 0RL, England

www.penguin.com

First published in the United States of America by The New Press, New York 2013
First published in Great Britain in Penguin Books 2014
008

ISBN: 978-0-241-96960-1

www.greenpenguin.co.uk

CONTENTS

INTRODUCTION

Anarcho-Curious?
or, Anarchist Amnesia

Nathan Schneider

The first evening of a solidarity bus tour in the West Bank, I listened as a contingent of college students from around the United States made an excellent discovery: they were all, at least kind of, anarchists. As they sat on stuffed chairs in the lobby of a lonely hotel near the refugee camp in war-ravaged Jenin, they probed one another's political tendencies, which were reflected in their ways of dressing and their most recent tattoos. All of this, along with stories of past trauma, made their way out into the light over the course of our ten-day trip.

"I think I would call myself an anarchist," one admitted.

Then another jumped into the space this created: "Yeah, totally."

Basic agreement about various ideologies and idioms ensued—ableism, gender queerness, Zapatistas, black blocs, borders. The students took their near unison as an almost incalculable coincidence, though it was no such thing.

This was the fall of 2012, just after the one-year anniversary of Occupy Wall Street. A new generation of radicals had experienced a moment in the limelight and a sense of possibility—and had little clear idea about what to do next. They had participated in an uprising that aspired to organize horizontally, that refused to address its demands to the proper authority, and that, like other concurrent movements around the world, prided itself on the absence of particular leaders. One couldn't call the Occupy movement an anarchist phenomenon per se; though some of its originators were self-conscious and articulate anarchists, most who took part wouldn't describe their objectives that way. Still, the mode of being that Occupy swept so many people into with its temporary autonomous zones in public squares nevertheless left them feeling, as it was sometimes said, anarcho-curious.

The generation most activated by Occupy is one for which the Cold War means everything and nothing. We came to consciousness in a world where communism was a doomed proposition from the get-go, vanquished by our Reagan-esque grandfathers and manifestly genocidal to boot. Capitalism won fair and square: market forces *work*. A vaguer kind of socialism, such as what furnished the functional train systems that carried us on backpacking trips across Europe, still held some appeal. Yet the word "socialism" has been so thoroughly tarnished in the hegemonic sound bites of Fox News as to be obviously unusable politically. It's also the word Fox associates with Barack Obama, whom this generation's door-knocking helped elect but whose administration strengthened the corporate oligarchy, waged unaccountable robot wars, and imprisoned migrant workers and heroic whistleblowers at record rates. So much for "socialism."

Anarchism, then, is a corner backed into rather than a conscious choice—an apophatic last resort, and a fruitful one.

It permits being political outside the red-and-blue confines of what is normally referred to as "politics" in the United States, without being doomed to a major party's inevitable betrayal. We can affirm the values we've learned on the Internet— transparency, crowd-sourcing, freedom to, freedom from. We can be ourselves.

Anarchy is the political blank slate of the early twenty-first century. It is shorthand for an eternal now, for a chance to restart the clock. Nowhere is this more evident than in the anarchic online collective Anonymous, whose only qualification for membership is having effaced one's identity, history, origins, and responsibility.

This anarchist amnesia that has overtaken radical politics in the United States is a reflection of the amnesia in U.S. politics generally. With the exception of a few shared mythologies about our founding slaveholders and our most murderous wars, we like to imagine that everything we do is being done for the very first time. Such amnesia can be useful, because it lends a sensation of pioneering vitality to our undertakings that the rest of the history-heavy world seems to envy. But it also condemns us to forever reinvent the wheel. And this means missing out on what makes anarchism worth taking seriously in the end: the prospect of learning, over the course of generations, how to build a well-organized and free society from the ground up.

Our capacity to forget is astonishing. In 1999, a horizontal "spokes council" organized the protests that helped shut down the World Trade Organization meeting in Seattle. Just over a decade later, a critical mass of Occupy Wall Street participants considered such a decision-making structure an illegitimate and intolerably reformist innovation.

Despite whatever extent to which we have ourselves to blame for our amnesia, however, it also has been imposed on us through repression against the threat anarchism was once perceived to pose. Remember that an American president was killed by an anarchist, and another anarchist assassination set off World War I. There are still unmarked gashes on buildings along Wall Street left over from anarchist bombs. More usefully, and more dangerously, anarchists used to travel across the country teaching industrial workers how to organize themselves and demand a fair share from their robber-baron bosses. Thus, the official questionnaire at Ellis Island sought to single out anarchists coming from Europe. Thus, Italian anarchists Sacco and Vanzetti were martyred in 1927, and roving grand juries imprison anarchists without charge today. Thus, we see liberal sleights of hand such as the one described in chapter 3, by which the anarchist popular revolution under way during the Spanish Civil War was deftly erased from history.

Anarchism's slate is really anything but blank. In this book Noam Chomsky plays the role of an ambassador for the kind of anarchism that we're supposed to have forgotten—that has a history and knows it, that has already shown another kind of world to be possible. He first encountered anarchism as a child in New York, before World War II succeeded in making capitalist-against-communist Manichaeism the unquestioned civil religion of the United States. He could find not just Marx but also Bakunin in the book stalls. He witnessed a capitalist class save itself from Depression-era ruin only by creating a social safety net and tolerating unions. The Zionism he was exposed to was a call to agrarian collectivism, not to military occupation.

The principle with which Chomsky describes his own anarchist leanings draws a common thread from early modern libertarian theorists like Godwin and Proudhon to the assassins of the early 1900s and the instincts of Anonymous today: power that isn't really justified by the will of the governed should be dismantled. More to the point, it should be refashioned from below. Without greedy elites maintaining their privilege with propaganda and force, workers might own and govern their workplaces, and communities might provide for the basic needs of everyone. Not all anarchist tactics are equally ethical or effective, but they do more or less arise from this common hope.

Into old age, Chomsky carries his anarchism with uncommon humaneness, without the need to put it on display as a black-masked caricature of itself. A lifetime of radical ideas and busy activism is enough of a credential. He sees no contradiction between holding anarchist ideals and pursuing certain reforms through the state when there's a chance for a more free, more just society in the short term; such humility is a necessary antidote to the self-defeating purism of many anarchists today. He represents a time when anarchists were truly fearsome—less because they were willing to put a brick through a Starbucks window than because they had figured out how to organize themselves in a functional, egalitarian, and sufficiently productive society.

This side of anarchism was the cause of George Orwell's revelry upon arriving in Barcelona to join the war against Franco. It's a moment he records in *Homage to Catalonia*, a book you'll find quoted several times in the pages that follow; already farms, factories, utilities, and militias were being run by workers along anarcho-socialist lines. Orwell recalls:

I had dropped more or less by chance into the only community of any size in Western Europe where political consciousness and disbelief in capitalism were more normal than their opposites. Up here in Aragon one was among tens of thousands of people, mainly though not entirely of working-class origin, all living at the same level and mingling on terms of equality. In theory it was perfect equality, and even in practice it was not far from it. There is a sense in which it would be true to say that one was experiencing a foretaste of Socialism, by which I mean that the prevailing mental atmosphere was that of Socialism. Many of the normal motives of civilized life—snobbishness, money-grubbing, fear of the boss, etc.— had simply ceased to exist. The ordinary class-division of society had disappeared to an extent that is almost unthinkable in the money-tainted air of England; there was no one there except the peasants and ourselves, and no one owned anyone else as his master. Of course such a state of affairs could not last. It was simply a temporary and local phase in an enormous game that is being played over the whole surface of the earth. But it lasted long enough to have its effect upon anyone who experienced it. However much one cursed at the time, one realized afterwards that one had been in contact with something strange and valuable. One had been in a community where hope was more normal than apathy or cynicism, where the word "comrade" stood for comradeship and not, as in most countries, for humbug. One had breathed the air of equality.

With a few proper nouns adjusted, much the same statement could have come from a witness to the Occupy movement, though the awe would be less well deserved. Orwell saw anarchy overtake a whole city along with large swaths of countryside, rather than the square block or less of a typical Occupy encampment. That these far smaller utopias managed to convey the same sense of knock-you-down newness, of soul-conquering significance, is probably because of historical amnesia again: most people had never learned about the bigger ones in school. They were astonished by the systematic violence used to eliminate the Occupy encampments because they hadn't heard about how the Spanish anarchists and the Paris Commune were crushed with military force as well. Amnesia constrains ambition and inoculates against patience.

Still, developments are under way that contribute to anarchism's legacy. Anarchists in this country now insist on grappling with challenges of sexual identity and ingrained oppression that mainstream society gingerly prefers not to recognize. They are at the forefront of movements to protect animal rights and the environment that future generations will be grateful for. As industrial agriculture becomes more and more poisoned by profit motives, anarchists are growing their own food. Anarchist hackers understand better than most of us the power of information and the lengths that those in power will go to control it; proof is in the years- and decades-long prison sentences now being doled out for online civil disobedience.

These mighty insights, along with so much else, risk being lost to amnesia if they're not passed on in memory and habit, if they're not treated as part of a legacy rather than as just passing reactions against the latest brand of crisis. At least in their various collectives and affinity groups, committed anarchists today tend to be a literate bunch who do know their history, even if others have forgotten.

A bit of historical consciousness suggests something else: there may be more anarcho-curiosity among us than we tend to realize. Among the supporting characters one finds in Peter Marshall's Chomsky-endorsed study *Demanding the Impossible: A History of Anarchism* are forefathers to those we call "libertarians" in the United States—which is to say, capitalists in favor of minimal government—including John Stuart Mill, Wilhelm von Humboldt, and Herbert Spencer.

Chomsky refers to right-wing libertarianism as "an aberration" nearly unique to this country, a theory of "a world built on hatred" that "would self-destruct in three seconds." Yet the vitality of this once- or twice-removed cousin of anarchism becomes evident with every election cycle, when libertarian candidate Ron Paul squeezes his way into the Republican debates thanks to the impressively determined and youthful "army" fighting for his "rEVOLution." (The capitalized words spell "LOVE" backward.) This is anarchism with corporate funding and misplaced nostalgia, its solidarity cleaved off by the willful protagonists in Ayn Rand's novels. Yet I'm more optimistic than I'm often told I should be about the prospects for and longings of this bloc and of the chances for reuniting it with a libertarianism more worth having.

In the early days and weeks of Occupy Wall Street, libertarian foot soldiers were out in force. They too had a bone to pick with a government-slash-empire that acts like a subsidiary of the big banks, and they kept trying to draw Occupiers into their sieges of the Federal Reserve building a block from occupied Zuccotti Park. But over time they withdrew from the encampments, probably after having had enough of the disorderliness and the leftist identity politics. They retreated to tabling stations a block or two away and then disappeared from the movement just about entirely.

The scenario could have played out differently. If it had, what might these right and left libertarianisms—equally amnesiac about their common origins—learn from one another?

The anarcho-curious left might rediscover that there is more to a functional resistance movement than youthful rebellion. Its members might, for instance, study working examples of the mutual aid they long for—education, material support, free day care—in churches and megachurches across the country, which form both the social life and the power base of the right. Independent of the state, these citadels put into practice something anarchists have been saying all along: no form of politics is worth our time until it helps struggling people get what they need, sustainably and reliably. All the better if you can do so without patriarchy and fundamentalism.

Meanwhile, the libertarian right might find the wherewithal to detach from its overly rosy view of the Constitution, from its more or less subtle racism against nonwhites and immigrants, and from its 1-percenter sponsors. It might raise tougher questions about whether "competition" is really the most liberating response to long-standing injustices along lines of gender, race, and circumstance. What would these young, energetic libertarians think if they encountered an egalitarian, democratic anarchism in the form of a robust political philosophy and practice? For too many people, Ayn Rand is as close to it as they are ever exposed to, and she's not very close at all.

Anarchism deserves better than to be a mere curiosity, or a blank slate, or an overlapping consensus among newly minted radicals who have trouble agreeing on anything else.

It is better than that. Both the anarcho-curiosity awakened by Occupy and the flourishing of right-wing libertarianism are signs that anarchism is overdue for recognition as a serious intellectual tradition and a real possibility. Noam Chomsky has been treating it that way throughout his career, and more of us should follow suit.

ON ANARCHISM

1

Notes on Anarchism

A French writer, sympathetic to anarchism, wrote in the 1890s that "anarchism has a broad back, like paper it endures anything"—including, he noted, those whose acts are such that "a mortal enemy of anarchism could not have done better."[1] There have been many styles of thought and action that have been referred to as "anarchist." It would be hopeless to try to encompass all of these conflicting tendencies in some general theory or ideology. And even if we proceed to extract from the history of libertarian thought a living, evolving tradition, as Daniel Guérin does in *Anarchism*, it remains difficult to formulate its doctrines as a specific and determinate theory of society and social change. The anarchist historian Rudolf Rocker, who presents a systematic conception of the development of anarchist thought towards anarchosyndicalism, along lines that bear comparison to Guérin's work, puts the matter well when he writes that anarchism is not

> a fixed, self-enclosed social system but rather a definite trend in the historic development of mankind, which, in contrast with the intellectual guardianship of all clerical and

governmental institutions, strives for the free unhindered unfolding of all the individual and social forces in life. Even freedom is only a relative, not an absolute concept, since it tends constantly to become broader and to affect wider circles in more manifold ways. For the anarchist, freedom is not an abstract philosophical concept, but the vital concrete possibility for every human being to bring to full development all the powers, capacities, and talents with which nature has endowed him, and turn them to social account. The less this natural development of man is influenced by ecclesiastical or political guardianship, the more efficient and harmonious will human personality become, the more will it become the measure of the intellectual culture of the society in which it has grown.[2]

One might ask what value there is in studying a "definite trend in the historic development of mankind" that does not articulate a specific and detailed social theory. Indeed, many commentators dismiss anarchism as utopian, formless, primitive, or otherwise incompatible with the realities of a complex society. One might, however, argue rather differently: that at every stage of history our concern must be to dismantle those forms of authority and oppression that survive from an era when they might have been justified in terms of the need for security or survival or economic development, but that now contribute to—rather than alleviate—material and cultural deficit. If so, there will be no doctrine of social change fixed for the present and future, nor even, necessarily, a specific and unchanging concept of the goals towards which social change should tend. Surely our understanding of the nature of man or of the range of viable social forms is so rudimentary that any far-reaching doctrine must be treated with great skepticism, just as skepticism is in order when we hear that "human nature" or "the demands of efficiency" or "the complexity of modern life" requires this or that form of oppression and autocratic rule.

Nevertheless, at a particular time there is every reason to develop, insofar as our understanding permits, a specific realization of this definite trend in the historic development of mankind, appropriate to the tasks of the moment. For Rocker, "the problem that is set for our time is that of freeing man from the curse of economic exploitation and political and social enslavement"; and the method is not the conquest and exercise of state power, nor stultifying parliamentarianism, but rather "to reconstruct the economic life of the peoples from the ground up and build it up in the spirit of Socialism."

> But only the producers themselves are fitted for this task, since they are the only value-creating element in society out of which a new future can arise. Theirs must be the task of freeing labor from all the fetters which economic exploitation has fastened on it, of freeing society from all the institutions and procedure of political power, and of opening the way to an alliance of free groups of men and women based on co-operative labor and a planned administration of things in the interest of the community. To prepare the toiling masses in city and country for this great goal and to bind them together as a militant force is the objective of modern Anarcho-syndicalism, and in this its whole purpose is exhausted. [p. 108]

As a socialist, Rocker would take for granted "that the serious, final, complete liberation of the workers is possible only upon one condition: that of the appropriation of capital, that is, of raw material and all the tools of labor, including land, by the whole body of the workers."[3] As an anarchosyndicalist, he insists, further, that the workers' organizations create "not only the ideas, but also the facts of the future itself" in the prerevolutionary period, that they embody in themselves the structure of the future society—and he looks forward to a social revolution that will dismantle the state apparatus as well as expropriate the expropriators. "What we put in place of the government is industrial organization."

> Anarcho-syndicalists are convinced that a Socialist economic order cannot be created by the decrees and statutes of a government, but only by the solidaric collaboration of the workers with hand and brain in each special branch of production; that is, through the taking over of the management of all plants by the producers themselves under such form that the separate groups, plants, and branches of industry are independent members of the general economic organism and systematically carry on production and the distribution of the products in the interest of the community on the basis of free mutual agreements. [p. 94]

Rocker was writing at a moment when such ideas had been put into practice in a dramatic way in the Spanish Revolution. Just prior to the outbreak of the revolution, the anarchosyndicalist economist Diego Abad de Santillan had written:

> . . . in facing the problem of social transformation, the Revolution cannot consider the state as a medium, but must depend on the organization of producers.

We have followed this norm and we find no need for the hypothesis of a superior power to organized labor, in order to establish a new order of things. We would thank anyone to point out to us what function, if any, the State can have in an economic organization, where private property has been abolished and in which parasitism and special privilege have no place. The suppression of the State cannot be a languid affair; it must be the task of the Revolution to finish with the State. Either the Revolution gives social wealth to the producers in which case the producers organize themselves for due collective distribution and the State has nothing to do; or the Revolution does not give social wealth to the producers, in which case the Revolution has been a lie and the State would continue.

Our federal council of economy is not a political power but an economic and administrative regulating power. It receives its orientation from below and operates in accordance with the resolutions of the regional and national assemblies. It is a liaison corps and nothing else.[4]

Engels, in a letter of 1883, expressed his disagreement with this conception as follows:

The anarchists put the thing upside down. They declare that the proletarian revolution must *begin* by doing away with the political organization of the state. . . . But to destroy it at such a moment would be to destroy the only organism by means of which the victorious proletariat can assert its newly-conquered power, hold down its capitalist adversaries, and carry out that economic revolution of society without which the whole

victory must end in a new defeat and in a mass slaughter of the
workers similar to those after the Paris commune.[5]

In contrast, the anarchists—most eloquently Bakunin—
warned of the dangers of the "red bureaucracy," which would
prove to be "the most vile and terrible lie that our century has
created."[6] The anarchosyndicalist Fernand Pelloutier asked:
"Must even the transitory state to which we have to submit
necessarily and fatally be the collectivist jail? Can't it consist
in a free organization limited exclusively by the needs of
production and consumption, all political institutions having
disappeared?"[7]

I do not pretend to know the answer to this question. But
it seems clear that unless there is, in some form, a positive
answer, the chances for a truly democratic revolution that will
achieve the humanistic ideals of the left are not great. Martin
Buber put the problem succinctly when he wrote: "One cannot in the nature of things expect a little tree that has been
turned into a club to put forth leaves."[8] The question of conquest or destruction of state power is what Bakunin regarded as
the primary issue dividing him from Marx.[9] In one form or another, the problem has arisen repeatedly in the century since,
dividing "libertarian" from "authoritarian" socialists.

Despite Bakunin's warnings about the red bureaucracy, and
their fulfillment under Stalin's dictatorship, it would obviously
be a gross error in interpreting the debates of a century ago
to rely on the claims of contemporary social movements as to
their historical origins. In particular, it is perverse to regard
Bolshevism as "Marxism in practice." Rather, the left-wing critique of Bolshevism, taking account of the historical circumstances of the Russian Revolution, is far more to the point.[10]

The anti-Bolshevik, left-wing labor movement opposed the Leninists because they did not go far enough in exploiting the Russian upheavals for strictly proletarian ends. They became prisoners of their environment and used the international radical movement to satisfy specifically Russian needs, which soon became synonymous with the needs of the Bolshevik Party-State. The "bourgeois" aspects of the Russian Revolution were now discovered in Bolshevism itself: Leninism was adjudged a part of international social-democracy, differing from the latter only on tactical issues.[11]

If one were to seek a single leading idea within the anarchist tradition, it should, I believe, be that expressed by Bakunin when, in writing on the Paris Commune, he identified himself as follows:

I am a fanatic lover of liberty, considering it as the unique condition under which intelligence, dignity and human happiness can develop and grow; not the purely formal liberty conceded, measured out and regulated by the State, an eternal lie which in reality represents nothing more than the privilege of some founded on the slavery of the rest; not the individualistic, egoistic, shabby, and fictitious liberty extolled by the School of J.-J. Rousseau and the other schools of bourgeois liberalism, which considers the would-be rights of all men, represented by the State which limits the rights of each—an idea that leads inevitably to the reduction of the rights of each to zero. No, I mean the only kind of liberty that is worthy of the name, liberty that consists in the full development of all of the material, intellectual and moral powers that are latent in each person; liberty that recognizes no restrictions other than those determined by the laws of our own individual nature, which cannot properly be regarded as restrictions since these laws are not imposed by any outside legislator beside or above us, but are immanent and inherent, forming the very basis of our material, intellectual and moral being—they do not limit us but are the real and immediate conditions of our freedom.[12]

These ideas grow out of the Enlightenment; their roots are in Rousseau's *Discourse on Inequality*, Humboldt's *Limits of State Action*, Kant's insistence, in his defense of the French Revolution, that freedom is the precondition for acquiring the maturity for freedom, not a gift to be granted when such maturity is achieved. With the development of industrial capitalism, a new and unanticipated system of injustice, it is libertarian socialism that has preserved and extended the radical humanist message of the Enlightenment and the classical liberal ideals that were perverted into an ideology to sustain the emerging social order. In fact, on the very same assumptions that led classical liberalism to oppose the intervention of the state in social life, capitalist social relations are also intolerable. This is clear, for example, from the classic work of Humboldt, *The Limits of State Action*, which anticipated and perhaps inspired Mill and to which we return below. This classic of liberal thought, completed in 1792, is in its essence profoundly, though prematurely, anticapitalist. Its ideas must be attenuated beyond recognition to be transmuted into an ideology of industrial capitalism.

Humboldt's vision of a society in which social fetters are replaced by social bonds and labor is freely undertaken suggests the early Marx, with his discussion of the "alienation of labor when work is external to the worker . . . not part of his nature . . . [so that] he does not fulfill himself in his work but denies himself . . . [and is] physically exhausted and mentally debased," alienated labor that "casts some of the workers back into a barbarous kind of work and turns others into machines," thus depriving man of his "species character" of "free conscious activity" and "productive life." Similarly, Marx conceives of "a new type of human being who *needs* his fellow-men. . . . [The workers' association becomes] the real constructive effort to create the social texture of future human relations."[13] It is true that classical libertarian thought is opposed to state intervention in social life, as a consequence of deeper assumptions about the human need for liberty, diversity, and free association. On the same assumptions, capitalist relations of production, wage labor, competitiveness, the ideology of "possessive individualism"—all must be regarded as fundamentally antihuman. Libertarian socialism is properly to be regarded as the inheritor of the liberal ideals of the Enlightenment.

Rudolf Rocker describes modern anarchism as "the confluence of the two great currents which during and since the French revolution have found such characteristic expression in the intellectual life of Europe: Socialism and Liberalism." The classical liberal ideals, he argues, were wrecked on the realities of capitalist economic forms. Anarchism is necessarily anticapitalist in that it "opposes the exploitation of man by man." But anarchism also opposes "the dominion of man over man." It insists that "*socialism will be free or it will not be at all.* In its recognition of this lies the genuine and profound justification for the existence of anarchism."[14] From this point of view, anarchism may be regarded as the libertarian wing of socialism.

It is in this spirit that Daniel Guérin has approached the study of anarchism in *Anarchism* and other works.[15]

Guérin quotes Adolph Fischer, who said that "every anarchist is a socialist but not every socialist is necessarily an anarchist." Similarly Bakunin, in his "anarchist manifesto" of 1865, the program of his projected international revolutionary fraternity, laid down the principle that each member must be, to begin with, a socialist.

A consistent anarchist must oppose private ownership of the means of production and the wage slavery which is a component of this system, as incompatible with the principle that labor must be freely undertaken and under the control of the producer. As Marx put it, socialists look forward to a society in which labor will "become not only a means of life, but also the highest want in life,"[16] an impossibility when the worker is driven by external authority or need rather than inner impulse: "no form of wage-labor, even though one may be less obnoxious than another, can do away with the misery of wage-labor itself."[17] A consistent anarchist must oppose not only alienated labor but also the stupefying specialization of labor that takes place when the means for developing production

> mutilate the worker into a fragment of a human being, degrade him to become a mere appurtenance of the machine, make his work such a torment that its essential meaning is destroyed; estrange from him the intellectual potentialities of the labor process in very proportion to the extent to which science is incorporated into it as an independent power. . . . [18]

Marx saw this not as an inevitable concomitant of industrialization, but rather as a feature of capitalist relations of production. The society of the future must be concerned to "replace the detail-worker of today . . . reduced to a mere fragment of a man, by the fully developed individual, fit for a variety of labours . . . to whom the different social functions . . . are but so many modes of giving free scope to his own natural powers."[19] The prerequisite is the abolition of capital and wage labor as social categories (not to speak of the industrial armies of the "labor state" or the various modern forms of totalitarianism or state capitalism). The reduction of man to an appurtenance of the machine, a specialized tool of production, might in principle be overcome, rather than enhanced, with the proper development and use of technology, but not under the conditions of autocratic control of production by those who make man an instrument to serve their ends, overlooking his individual purposes, in Humboldt's phrase.

Anarchosyndicalists sought, even under capitalism, to create "free associations of free producers" that would engage in militant struggle and prepare to take over the organization of production on a democratic basis. These associations would serve as "a practical school of anarchism."[20] If private ownership of the means of production is, in Proudhon's often quoted phrase, merely a form of "theft"—"the exploitation of the weak by the strong"[21]—control of production by a state bureaucracy, no matter how benevolent its intentions, also does not create the conditions under which labor, manual and intellectual, can become the highest want in life. Both, then, must be overcome.

In his attack on the right of private or bureaucratic control over the means of production, the anarchist takes his stand with those who struggle to bring about "the third and last emancipatory phase of history," the first having made serfs out of slaves, the second having made wage earners out of serfs, and the third which abolishes the proletariat in a final act of liberation that places control over the economy in the hands of free and voluntary associations of producers (Fourier, 1848).[22] The imminent danger to "civilization" was noted by de Tocqueville, also in 1848:

> As long as the right of property was the origin and groundwork of many other rights, it was easily defended—or rather it was not attacked; it was then the citadel of society while all the other rights were its outworks; it did not bear the brunt of attack and, indeed, there was no serious attempt to assail it. But today, when the right of property is regarded as the last undestroyed remnant of the aristocratic world, when it alone is left standing, the sole privilege in an equalized society, it is a different matter. Consider what is happening in the hearts of the working-classes, although I admit they are quiet as yet. It is true that they are less inflamed than formerly by political passions properly speaking; but do you not see that their passions, far from being political, have become social? Do you not see that, little by little, ideas and opinions are spreading amongst them which aim not merely at removing such and such laws, such a ministry or such a government, but at breaking up the very foundations of society itself?[23]

The workers of Paris, in 1871, broke the silence, and proceeded

> to abolish property, the basis of all civilization! Yes, gentlemen, the Commune intended to abolish that class property which makes the labor of the many the wealth of the few. It aimed at the expropriation of the expropriators. It wanted to

make individual property a truth by transforming the means of production, land and capital, now chiefly the means of enslaving and exploiting labor, into mere instruments of free and associated labor.[24]

The Commune, of course, was drowned in blood. The nature of the "civilization" that the workers of Paris sought to overcome in their attack on "the very foundations of society itself" was revealed, once again, when the troops of the Versailles government reconquered Paris from its population. As Marx wrote, bitterly but accurately:

> The civilization and justice of bourgeois order comes out in its lurid light whenever the slaves and drudges of that order rise against their masters. Then this civilization and justice stand forth as undisguised savagery and lawless revenge . . . the infernal deeds of the soldiery reflect the innate spirit of that civilization of which they are the mercenary vindicators. . . . The bourgeoisie of the whole world, which looks complacently upon the wholesale massacre after the battle, is convulsed by horror at the desecration of brick and mortar. [Ibid., pp. 74, 77]

Despite the violent destruction of the Commune, Bakunin wrote that Paris opens a new era, "that of the definitive and complete emancipation of the popular masses and their future true solidarity, across and despite state boundaries . . . the next revolution of man, international and in solidarity, will be the resurrection of Paris"—a revolution that the world still awaits.

The consistent anarchist, then, should be a socialist, but a socialist of a particular sort. He will not only oppose alienated and specialized labor and look forward to the appropriation of capital by the whole body of workers, but he will also insist that this appropriation be direct, not exercised by some elite force acting in the name of the proletariat. He will, in short, oppose

> the organization of production by the Government. It means State-socialism, the command of the State officials over production and the command of managers, scientists, shop-officials in the shop. . . . The goal of the working class is liberation from exploitation. This goal is not reached and cannot be reached by a new directing and governing class substituting itself for the bourgeoisie. It is only realized by the workers themselves being master over production.

These remarks are taken from "Five Theses on the Class Struggle" by the left-wing Marxist Anton Pannekoek, one of the outstanding theorists of the council communist movement. And in fact, radical Marxism merges with anarchist currents.

As a further illustration, consider the following characterization of "revolutionary Socialism":

> The revolutionary Socialist denies that State ownership can end in anything other than a bureaucratic despotism. We have seen why the State cannot democratically control industry. Industry can only be democratically owned and controlled by the workers electing directly from their own ranks industrial administrative committees. Socialism will be fundamentally an industrial system; its constituencies will be of an industrial character. Thus those carrying on the social activities and industries of society will be directly represented in the local and central councils of social administration. In this way the

powers of such delegates will flow upwards from those carrying on the work and conversant with the needs of the community. When the central administrative industrial committee meets it will represent every phase of social activity. Hence the capitalist political or geographical state will be replaced by the industrial administrative committee of Socialism. The transition from the one social system to the other will be the *social revolution*. The political State throughout history has meant the government *of men* by ruling classes; the Republic of Socialism will be the government of *industry* administered on behalf of the whole community. The former meant the economic and political subjection of the many; the latter will mean the economic freedom of all—it will be, therefore, a true democracy.

This programmatic statement appears in William Paul's *The State, Its Origins and Function*, written in early 1917—shortly before Lenin's *State and Revolution*, perhaps his most libertarian work (see note 9). Paul was a member of the Marxist–De Leonist Socialist Labor Party and later one of the founders of the British Communist Party.[25] His critique of state socialism resembles the libertarian doctrine of the anarchists in its principle that since state ownership and management will lead to bureaucratic despotism, the social revolution must replace it by the industrial organization of society with direct workers' control. Many similar statements can be cited.

What is far more important is that these ideas have been realized in spontaneous revolutionary action, for example in Germany and Italy after World War I and in Spain (not only in the agricultural countryside, but also in industrial Barcelona) in 1936. One might argue that some form of council communism is the natural form of revolutionary socialism in an industrial society. It reflects the intuitive understanding that democracy is severely limited when the industrial system is controlled by any form of autocratic elite, whether of owners, managers and technocrats, a "vanguard" party, or a state bureaucracy. Under these conditions of authoritarian domination the classical libertarian ideals developed further by Marx and Bakunin and all true revolutionaries cannot be realized; man will not be free to develop his own potentialities to their fullest, and the producer will remain "a fragment of a human being," degraded, a tool in the productive process directed from above.

The phrase "spontaneous revolutionary action" can be misleading. The anarchosyndicalists, at least, took very seriously Bakunin's remark that the workers' organizations must create "not only the ideas but also the facts of the future itself" in the prerevolutionary period. The accomplishments of the popular revolution in Spain, in particular, were based on the patient work of many years of organization and education, one component of a long tradition of commitment and militancy. The resolutions of the Madrid Congress of June 1931 and the Saragossa Congress in May 1936 foreshadowed in many ways the acts of the revolution, as did the somewhat different ideas sketched by Santillan (see note 4) in his fairly specific account of the social and economic organization to be instituted by the revolution. Guérin writes: "The Spanish revolution was relatively mature in the minds of the libertarian thinkers, as in the popular consciousness." And workers' organizations existed with the structure, the experience, and the understanding to undertake the task of social reconstruction when, with the Franco coup, the turmoil of early 1936 exploded into social revolution. In his introduction to a collection of documents on collectivization in Spain, the anarchist Augustin Souchy writes:

> For many years, the anarchists and syndicalists of Spain considered their supreme task to be the social transformation of the society. In their assemblies of Syndicates and groups, in their journals, their brochures and books, the problem of the social revolution was discussed incessantly and in a systematic fashion.[26]

All of this lies behind the spontaneous achievements, the constructive work of the Spanish Revolution.

The ideas of libertarian socialism, in the sense described, have been submerged in the industrial societies of the past half-century. The dominant ideologies have been those of state socialism or state capitalism (of an increasingly militarized character in the United States, for reasons that are not obscure).[27] But there has been a rekindling of interest in the past few years. The theses I quoted by Anton Pannekoek were taken from a recent pamphlet of a radical French workers' group (*Informations Correspondance Ouvrière*). The remarks by William Paul on revolutionary socialism are cited in a paper by Walter Kendall given at the National Conference on Workers' Control in Sheffield, England, in March 1969. The workers' control movement has become a significant force in England in the past few years. It has organized several conferences and has produced a substantial pamphlet literature, and counts among its active adherents representatives of some of the most important trade unions. The Amalgamated Engineering and Foundryworkers' Union, for example, has adopted, as official

policy, the program of nationalization of basic industries under "workers' control at all levels."[28] On the Continent, there
are similar developments. May 1968 of course accelerated the
growing interest in council communism and related ideas in
France and Germany, as it did in England.

Given the general conservative cast of our highly ideological society, it is not too surprising that the United States has
been relatively untouched by these developments. But that too
may change. The erosion of the cold-war mythology at least
makes it possible to raise these questions in fairly broad circles.
If the present wave of repression can be beaten back, if the left
can overcome its more suicidal tendencies and build upon
what has been accomplished in the past decade, then the problem of how to organize industrial society on truly democratic
lines, with democratic control in the workplace and in the
community, should become a dominant intellectual issue for
those who are alive to the problems of contemporary society,
and, as a mass movement for libertarian socialism develops,
speculation should proceed to action.

In his manifesto of 1865, Bakunin predicted that one element in the social revolution will be "that intelligent and truly
noble part of the youth which, though belonging by birth to
the privileged classes, in its generous convictions and ardent
aspirations, adopts the cause of the people." Perhaps in the rise
of the student movement of the 1960s one sees steps towards a
fulfillment of this prophecy.

Daniel Guérin has undertaken what he has described as
a "process of rehabilitation" of anarchism. He argues, con-
vincingly I believe, that "the constructive ideas of anarchism
retain their vitality, that they may, when re-examined and
sifted, assist contemporary socialist thought to undertake a

new departure . . . [and] contribute to enriching Marxism."[29] From the "broad back" of anarchism he has selected for more intensive scrutiny those ideas and actions that can be described as libertarian socialist. This is natural and proper. This framework accommodates the major anarchist spokesmen as well as the mass actions that have been animated by anarchist sentiments and ideals. Guérin is concerned not only with anarchist thought but also with the spontaneous actions of popular forces that actually create new social forms in the course of revolutionary struggle. He is concerned with social as well as intellectual creativity. Furthermore, he attempts to draw from the constructive achievements of the past lessons that will enrich the theory of social liberation. For those who wish not only to understand the world, but also to change it, this is the proper way to study the history of anarchism.

Guérin describes the anarchism of the nineteenth century as essentially doctrinal, while the twentieth century, for the anarchists, has been a time of "revolutionary practice."[30] *Anarchism* reflects that judgment. His interpretation of anarchism consciously points towards the future. Arthur Rosenberg once pointed out that popular revolutions characteristically seek to replace "a feudal or centralized authority ruling by force" with some form of communal system which "implies the destruction and disappearance of the old form of State." Such a system will be either socialist or an "extreme form of democracy . . . [which is] the preliminary condition for Socialism inasmuch as Socialism can only be realized in a world enjoying the highest possible measure of individual freedom." This idea, he notes, was common to Marx and the anarchists.[31] This natural struggle for liberation runs counter to the prevailing tendency towards centralization in economic and political life.

A century ago Marx wrote that the bourgeosie of Paris "felt there was but one alternative—the Commune, or the empire—under whatever name it might reappear."

> The empire had ruined them economically by the havoc it made of public wealth, by the wholesale financial swindling it fostered, by the props it lent to the artificially accelerated centralization of capital, and the concomitant expropriation of their own ranks. It had suppressed them politically, it had shocked them morally by its orgies, it had insulted their Voltairianism by handing over the education of their children to the *frères Ignorantins*, it had revolted their national feeling as Frenchmen by precipitating them headlong into a war which left only one equivalent for the ruins it made—the disappearance of the empire.[32]

The miserable Second Empire "was the only form of government possible at a time when the bourgeoisie had already lost, and the working class had not yet acquired, the faculty of ruling the nation."

It is not very difficult to rephrase these remarks so that they become appropriate to the imperial systems of 1970. The problem of "freeing man from the curse of economic exploitation and political and social enslavement" remains the problem of our time. As long as this is so, the doctrines and the revolutionary practice of libertarian socialism will serve as an inspiration and a guide.

2

Excerpts from *Understanding Power*

TRANSCENDING CAPITALISM

MAN: *Referring back to your comments about escaping from or doing away with capitalism, I'm wondering what workable scheme you would put in its place?*

Me?

MAN: *Or what would you suggest to others who might be in a position to set it up and get it going?*

Well, I think that what used to be called, centuries ago, "wage slavery" is intolerable. I mean, I do not think that people ought to be forced to rent themselves in order to survive. I think that the economic institutions ought to be run democratically—by their participants, and by the communities in which they live.

The note references in this chapter were left intact to match the original note numbering. The editors' explanatory notes can be found online at understandingpower.com/chap6.htm.

And I think that through various forms of free association and federalism, it's possible to imagine a society working like that. I mean, I don't think you can lay it out in *detail*—nobody's smart enough to design a society; you've got to experiment. But reasonable principles on which to build such a society are quite clear.

MAN: *Most efforts at planned economies kind of go against the grain of democratic ideals, and founder on those rocks.*

Well, it depends which planned economies you mean. There are lots of planned economies—the United States is a planned economy, for example. I mean, we talk about ourselves as a "free market," but that's baloney. The only parts of the U.S. economy that are internationally competitive are the planned parts, the state-subsidized parts—like capital-intensive agriculture (which has a state-guaranteed market as a cushion in case there are excesses); or high-technology industry (which is dependent on the Pentagon system); or pharmaceuticals (which is massively subsidized by publicly funded research). Those are the parts of the U.S. economy that are functioning well.

And if you go to the East Asian countries that are supposed to be the big economic successes—you know, what everybody talks about as a triumph of free-market democracy—they don't even have the most remote relation to free-market democracy: formally speaking they're fascist, they're state-organized economies run in cooperation with big conglomerates. That's precisely fascism, it's not the free market.

Now, that kind of planned economy "works," in a way—it produces at least. Other kinds of command economies don't work, or work differently: for example, the Eastern European planned economies in the Soviet era were highly centralized, over-bureaucratized, and they worked very inefficiently, although they did provide a kind of minimal safety net for people. But all of these systems have been very antidemocratic—like, in the Soviet Union, there were virtually no peasants or workers involved in any decision-making process.

MAN: *It would be hard to find a working model of an ideal.*

Yes, but in the eighteenth century it would have been hard to find a working model of a political democracy—that didn't prove it couldn't exist. By the nineteenth century, it did exist. Unless you think that human history is over, it's not an argument to say "it's not around." You go back two hundred years, it was hard to imagine slavery being abolished.

THE KIBBUTZ EXPERIMENT

ANOTHER MAN: *How could you make decisions democratically without a bureaucracy? I don't see how a large mass of people could actively participate in all of the decisions that need to be made in a complex modern society.*

No, I don't think they can—I think you've got to delegate some of those responsibilities. But the question is, where does authority ultimately lie? I mean, since the very beginnings of the modern democratic revolutions in the seventeenth and eighteenth centuries, it's always been recognized that people have to be represented—the question is, are we represented by, as they put it, "countrymen like ourselves," or are we represented by "our betters?"

For example, suppose this was our community, and we wanted to enter into some kind of arrangement with the community down the road—if we were fairly big in scale, we couldn't *all* do it and get them *all* to do it, we'd have to del-egate the right to negotiate things to representatives. But then the question is, who has the power to ultimately authorize those decisions? Well, if it's a democracy, that power ought to lie not just *formally* in the population, but *actually* in the population—meaning the representatives can be recalled, they're answerable back to their community, they can be re-placed. In fact, there should be as much as possible in the way of constant replacement, so that political participation just becomes a part of everybody's life.

But I agree, I don't think it's possible to have large masses of people get together to decide every topic—it would be unfea-sible and pointless. You're going to want to pick committees to look into things and report back, and so on and so forth. But the real question is, where does authority lie?

MAN: *It sounds like the model you're looking to is similar to that of the kibbutzim [collective farming communities in Israel].*

Yeah, the kibbutz is actually as close to a full democracy as there is, I think. In fact, I lived on one for a while, and had planned to stay there, for precisely these reasons. On the other hand, life is full of all kinds of ironies, and the fact is—as I have come to understand over the years even more than I did at one time—although the kibbutzim are very authentic democracies internally, there are a lot of very ugly features about them.

For one thing, they're extremely racist: I don't think there's a single Arab on any kibbutz in Israel, and it turns out that a fair number of them have been turned down. Like, if a couple forms between a Jewish member of a kibbutz and an Arab, they generally end up living in an Arab village. The other thing about them is, they have an extremely unpleasant relationship with the state—which I didn't really know about until fairly recently, even though it's been that way for a long time.

See, part of the reason why the kibbutzim are economically successful is that they get a substantial state subsidy, and in return for that state subsidy they essentially provide the officers' corps for the elite military units in Israel. So if you look at who goes into the pilot training schools and the rangers and all that kind of stuff, it's kibbutz kids—that's the trade-off: the government subsidizes them as long as they provide the Praetorian Guard. Furthermore, I think they end up providing the Praetorian Guard in part as a result of kibbutz education. And here there are things that people who believe in libertarian ideas, as I do, really have to worry about.

You see, there's something very authoritarian about the libertarian structure of the kibbutz—I could see it when I lived in it, in fact. There's tremendous group pressure to conform. I mean, there's no force that *makes* you conform, but the group pressures are very powerful. The dynamics of how this worked were never very clear to me, but you could just see it in operation: the fear of exclusion is very great—not exclusion in the sense of not being allowed into the dining room or something, but just that you won't be a part of things somehow. It's like being excluded from a family: if you're a kid and your family excludes you—like maybe they let you sit at the table, but they don't talk to you—that's devastating, you just can't survive it. And something like that carries over into these communities.

I've never heard of anybody studying it, but if you watch the kids growing up, you can understand *why* they're going to go into the rangers and the pilot programs and the commandos. There's a tremendous macho pressure, right from the very beginning—you're just no good unless you can go through Marine Corps training and become a really tough bastard. And that starts pretty early, and I think the kids go through real traumas if they can't do it: it's psychologically very difficult.

And the results are striking. For example, there's a movement of resisters in Israel [Yesh G'vul], people who won't serve in the Occupied Territories—but it doesn't have any kibbutz kids in it: the movement just doesn't exist there. Kibbutz kids also have a reputation for being what are called "good soldiers"—which means, you know, not nice people: do what you gotta do. All of these things are other aspects of it, and the whole phenomenon comes pretty much without force or authority, but because of a dynamics of conformism that's extremely powerful.

Like, the kibbutz I lived in was made up of pretty educated people—they were German refugees, and a lot of them had university degrees and so on—but every single person in the whole kibbutz read the same newspaper. And the idea that you might read a different newspaper—well, it's not that there was a law against it, it was just that it couldn't be done: you're a member of *this* branch of the kibbutz movement, that's the newspaper you read.

MAN: *Then how can we build a social contract which is coop-*
erative in nature, but at the same time recognizes individual
humanity? It seems to me that there's always going to be a very
tense polar pull there.

Where's the polar pull—between what and what?

MAN: *Between a collective value and an individual value.*

I guess I don't see why there has to be any contradiction there
at all. It seems to me that a crucial aspect of humanity is being
a part of functioning communities—so if we can create social
bonds in which people find satisfaction, we've done it: there's
no contradiction.

Look, you can't really figure out what problems are going to
arise in group situations unless you experiment with them—it's
like physics: you can't just sit around and think what the world
would be like under such and such conditions, you've got to
experiment and learn how things actually work out. And one
of the things I think you learn from the kibbutz experiment is
that you can in fact construct quite viable and successful democratic structures—but there are still going to be problems that
come along. And one of the problems that people just have to
face is the effect of group pressures to conform.

I think everybody knows about this from families. Living
in a family is a crucial part of human life, you don't want to
give it up. On the other hand, there plainly are problems that
go along with it—nobody has to be told that. And a serious
problem, which becomes almost pathological when it arises in
a close-knit group, is exclusion—and to avoid exclusion often
means doing things you wouldn't want to do if you had your

own way. But that's just a part of living, to be faced with human problems like that.

Actually, I'm not a great enthusiast of Marx, but one comment he made seems appropriate here. I'm quoting, so pardon the sexist language, but somewhere or other he said: socialism is an effort to try to solve man's *animal* problems, and after having solved the animal problems, then we can face the *human* problems—but it's not a part of socialism to solve the human problems; socialism is an effort to get you to the point where you can *face* the human problems. And I think the kind of thing you're concerned about is a human problem—and those are going to be there. Humans are very complicated creatures, and have lots of ways of torturing themselves in their inter-personal relations. Everybody knows that, without soap operas.

"ANARCHISM" AND "LIBERTARIANISM"

WOMAN: *Professor Chomsky, on a slightly different topic, there's a separate meaning of the word "anarchy" different from the one you often talk about—namely, "chaos."*

Yeah, it's a bum rap, basically—it's like referring to Soviet-style bureaucracy as "socialism," or any other term of discourse that's been given a second meaning for the purpose of ideological warfare. I mean, "chaos" is a meaning of the word, but it's not a meaning that has any relevance to social thought. Anarchy as a social philosophy has never meant "chaos"—in fact, anarchists have typically believed in a highly organized society, just one that's organized democratically from below.

WOMAN: *It seems to me that as a social system, anarchism makes such bottom-line sense that it was necessary to discredit the word, and take it out of people's whole vocabulary and thinking—so you just have a reflex of fear when you hear it.*

Yeah, anarchism has always been regarded as the ultimate evil by people with power. So in Woodrow Wilson's Red Scare [a 1919 campaign against "subversives" in the U.S.], they were harsh on socialists, but they murdered anarchists—they were really bad news.

See, the idea that people could be free is extremely frightening to anybody with power. That's why the 1960s have such a bad reputation. I mean, there's a big literature about the Sixties, and it's mostly written by intellectuals, because they're the people who write books, so naturally it has a very bad name—because they *hated* it. You could see it in the faculty clubs at the time: people were just traumatized by the idea that students were suddenly asking questions and not just copying things down. In fact, when people like Allan Bloom [author of *The Closing of the American Mind*] write as if the foundations of civilization were collapsing in the Sixties, from their point of view that's exactly right: they were. Because the foundations of civilization are, "I'm a big professor, and I tell you what to say, and what to think, and you write it down in your notebooks, and you repeat it." If you get up and say, "I don't understand why I should read Plato, I think it's nonsense," that's destroying the foundations of civilization. But maybe it's a perfectly sensible question—plenty of philosophers have said it, so why isn't it a sensible question?

As with any mass popular movement, there was a lot of crazy stuff going on in the Sixties—but that's the only thing that makes it into history: the crazy stuff around the periphery. The main things that were going on are out of history—and that's because they had a kind of libertarian character, and there is nothing more frightening to people with power.

MAN: *What's the difference between "libertarian" and "anarchist," exactly?*

There's no difference, really. I think they're the same thing. But you see, "libertarian" has a special meaning in the United States. The United States is off the spectrum of the main tradition in this respect: what's called "libertarianism" here is unbridled capitalism. Now, that's always been opposed in the European libertarian tradition, where every anarchist has been a socialist—because the point is, if you have unbridled capitalism, you have all kinds of authority: you have *extreme* authority.

If capital is privately controlled, then people are going to have to rent themselves in order to survive. Now, you can say, "they rent themselves freely, it's a free contract"—but that's a joke. If your choice is, "do what I tell you or starve," that's not a choice—it's in fact what was commonly referred to as wage slavery in more civilized times, like the eighteenth and nineteenth centuries, for example.

The American version of "libertarianism" is an aberration, though—nobody really takes it seriously. I mean, everybody knows that a society that worked by American libertarian principles would self-destruct in three seconds. The only reason people pretend to take it seriously is because you can use it as a weapon. Like, when somebody comes out in favor of a tax, you can say: "No, I'm a libertarian, I'm against that tax"—but of course, I'm still in favor of the government building roads, and having schools, and killing Libyans, and all that sort of stuff.

Now, there *are* consistent libertarians, people like Murray Rothbard [American academic]—and if you just read the world that they describe, it's a world so full of hate that no human being would want to live in it. This is a world where you don't have roads because you don't see any reason why you should cooperate in building a road that you're not going to use: if you want a road, you get together with a bunch of other people who are going to use that road and you build it, then you charge people to ride on it. If you don't like the pollution from somebody's automobile, you take them to court and you litigate it. Who would want to live in a world like that? It's a world built on hatred.

The whole thing's not even worth talking about, though. First of all, it couldn't function for a second—and if it could, all you'd want to do is get out, or commit suicide or something. But this is a special American aberration, it's not really serious.

ARTICULATING VISIONS

MAN: *You often seem reluctant to get very specific in spelling out your vision of an anarchist society and how we could get there. Don't you think it's important for activists to do that, though—to try to communicate to people a workable plan for the future, which then can help give them the hope and energy to continue struggling? I'm curious why you don't do that more often.*

Well, I suppose I *don't* feel that in order to work hard for social change you need to be able to spell out a plan for a future society in any kind of detail. What I feel should drive a person to work for change are certain *principles* you'd like to see achieved. Now, you may not know in detail—and I don't think that any of us *do* know in detail—how those principles can best be realized at this point in complex systems like human societies. But I don't really see why that should make any difference: what you try to do is advance the principles. Now, that may be what some people call "reformism"—but that's kind of like a put-down: reforms can be quite revolutionary if they lead in a certain direction. And to push in that direction, I don't think you have to know precisely how a future society would work: I think what you have to be able to do is spell out the principles you want to see such a society realize—and I think we can imagine *many* different ways in which a future society could realize them. Well, work to help people start trying them.

So for example, in the case of workers taking control of the workplace, there are a lot of different ways in which you can think of workplaces being controlled—and since nobody knows enough about what all the effects are going to be of large-scale social changes, I think what we should do is try them piecemeal. In fact, I have a rather conservative attitude towards social change: since we're dealing with complex systems which nobody understands very much, the sensible move I think is to make changes and then see what happens—and if they work, make further changes. That's true across the board, actually.

So, I don't feel in a position—and even if I felt I was, I wouldn't say it—to know what the long-term results are going to look like in any kind of detail: those are things that will have to be discovered, in my view. Instead, the basic principle I would like to see communicated to people is the idea that every form of authority and domination and hierarchy, every authoritarian structure, has to prove that it's justified—it has no prior justification. For instance, when you stop your five-year-old kid from trying to cross the street, that's an authoritarian situation: it's got to be justified. Well, in that case, I think you *can* give a justification. But the burden of proof for any exercise of authority is always on the person exercising it—invariably. And when you look, most of the time these authority structures have no justification: they have no moral justification, they have no justification in the interests of the person lower in the hierarchy, or in the interests of other people, or the environment, or the future, or the society, or anything else—they're just there in order to preserve certain structures of power and domination, and the people at the top.

So I think that whenever you find situations of power, these questions should be asked—and the person who claims the legitimacy of the authority always bears the burden of justifying it. And if they can't justify it, it's illegitimate and should be dismantled. To tell you the truth, I don't really understand anarchism as being much more than that. As far as I can see, it's just the point of view that says that people have the right to be free, and if there are constraints on that freedom then you've got to justify them. Sometimes you can—but of course, anarchism or anything else doesn't give you the answers about when that is. You just have to look at the specific cases.

MAN: *But if we ever had a society with no wage incentive and no authority, where would the drive come from to advance and grow?*

Well, the drive to "advance"—I think you have to ask exactly what that means. If you mean a drive to *produce more*, well, who wants it? Is that necessarily the right thing to do? It's not obvious. In fact, in many areas it's probably the wrong thing to do—maybe it's a good thing that there wouldn't be the same drive to produce. People have to be *driven* to have certain wants in our system—why? Why not leave them alone so they can just be happy, do other things?

Whatever "drive" there is ought to be internal. So take a look at kids: they're creative, they explore, they want to try new things. I mean, why does a kid start to walk? You take a one-year-old kid, he's crawling fine, he can get anywhere across the room he likes really fast, so fast his parents have to run after him to keep him from knocking everything down—all of a sudden he gets up and starts walking. He's terrible at walking: he walks one step and he falls on his face, and if he wants to really get somewhere he's going to crawl. So why do kids start walking? Well, they just want to do new things, that's the way people are built. We're built to want to do new things, even if they're not efficient, even if they're harmful, even if you get hurt—and I don't think that ever stops.

People want to explore, we want to press our capacities to their limits, we want to appreciate what we can. But the joy of creation is something very few people get the opportunity to have in our society: artists get to have it, craftspeople have it, scientists. And if you've been lucky enough to have had that opportunity, you know it's quite an experience—and it doesn't have to be discovering Einstein's theory of relativity: anybody can have that pleasure, even by seeing what *other* people have done. For instance, if you read even a simple mathematical proof like the Pythagorean Theorem, what you study in tenth grade, and you finally figure out what it's all about, that's exciting—"My God, I never understood that before." Okay, that's creativity, even though somebody else proved it two thousand years ago.

You just keep being struck by the marvels of what you're discovering, and you're "discovering" it, even though somebody else did it already. Then if you can ever add a little bit to what's already known—alright, that's very exciting. And I think the same thing is true of a person who builds a boat: I don't see why it's fundamentally any different—I mean, I wish *I* could do that; I can't, I can't imagine doing it.

Well, I think people should be able to live in a society where they can exercise these kinds of internal drives and develop their capacities freely—instead of being forced into the narrow range of options that are available to most people in the world now. And by that, I mean not only options that are *objectively* available, but also options that are *subjectively* available—like, how are people allowed to think, how are they able to think? Remember, there are all kinds of ways of thinking that are cut off from us in our society—not because we're incapable of them, but because various blockages have been developed and imposed to prevent people from thinking in those ways. That's what indoctrination is *about* in the first place, in fact— and I don't mean somebody giving you lectures: sitcoms on television, sports that you watch, every aspect of the culture implicitly involves an expression of what a "proper" life and a "proper" set of values are, and that's all indoctrination.

So I think what has to happen is, other options have to be opened up to people—both subjectively, and in fact concretely: meaning you can do something about them without great suffering. And that's one of the main purposes of socialism, I think: to reach a point where people have the opportunity to decide freely for *themselves* what their needs are, and not just have the "choices" forced on them by some arbitrary system of power. [...]

ADAM SMITH: REAL AND FAKE

MAN: *You said that classical liberalism was "anticapitalist." What did you mean by that?*

Well, the underlying, fundamental principles of Adam Smith and other classical liberals were that people should be free: they shouldn't be under the control of authoritarian institutions, they shouldn't be subjected to things like division of labor, which destroys them. So look at Smith: why was he in favor of markets? He gave kind of a complicated argument for them, but at the core of it was the idea that if you had perfect liberty, markets would lead to perfect equality—that's why Adam Smith was in favor of markets. Adam Smith was in favor of markets because he thought that people ought to be completely equal—*completely equal*—and that was because, as a classical liberal, he believed that people's fundamental character involves notions like sympathy, and solidarity, the right to control their own work, and so on and so forth: all the exact opposite of capitalism.

In fact, there are no two points of view more antithetical than classical liberalism and capitalism—and that's why when the University of Chicago publishes a bicentennial edition of Smith, they have to distort the text (which they did): because as a true classical liberal, Smith was strongly opposed to all of the idiocy they now spout in his name.

So if you read George Stigler's introduction to the bicentennial edition of *The Wealth of Nations*—it's a big scholarly edition, University of Chicago Press, so it's kind of interesting to look at—it is diametrically opposed to Smith's text on point after point. Smith is famous for what he wrote about division of labor: he's supposed to have thought that division of labor was a great thing. Well, he didn't: he thought division of labor was a *terrible* thing—in fact, he said that in any civilized society, the government is going to have to intervene to prevent division of labor from simply destroying people. Okay, now take a look at the University of Chicago's index (you know, a detailed scholarly index) under "division of labor": you won't find an entry for that passage—it's simply not there.

Well, that's *real* scholarship: suppress the facts totally, present them as the opposite of what they are, and figure, "probably nobody's going to read to page 473 anyhow, because I didn't." I mean, ask the guys who edited it if *they* ever read to page 473—answer: well, they probably read the first paragraph, then sort of remembered what they'd been taught in some college course.

But the point is, for classical liberals in the eighteenth century, there was a certain conception of just what human beings are like—namely, that what kind of creatures they are depends on the kind of work they do, and the kind of control they have over it, and their ability to act creatively and according to their own decisions and choices. And there was in fact a lot of very insightful comment about this at the time.

So for example, one of the founders of classical liberalism, Wilhelm von Humboldt (who incidentally is very admired by so-called "conservatives" today, because they don't read him), pointed out that if a worker produces a beautiful object on command, you may "admire what the worker does, but you will despise what he is"—because that's not really behaving like a human being, it's just behaving like a machine. And that conception runs right through classical liberalism. In fact, even half a century later, Alexis de Tocqueville [French politician and writer] pointed out that you can have systems in which "the art advances and the artisan recedes," but that's inhuman—because what you're really interested in is the artisan, you're interested in *people*, and for people to have the opportunity to live full and rewarding lives they have to be in control of what they do, even if that happens to be economically less efficient.

Well, okay—obviously there's just been a dramatic change in intellectual and cultural attitudes over the past couple centuries. But I think those classical liberal conceptions now have to be recovered, and the ideas at the heart of them should take root on a mass scale.

Now, the sources of power and authority that people could see in front of their eyes in the eighteenth century were quite different from the ones that we have today—back then it was the feudal system, and the Church, and the absolutist state that they were focused on; they couldn't see the industrial corporation, because it didn't exist yet. But if you take the basic classical liberal principles and apply them to the modern period, I think you actually come pretty close to the principles that animated revolutionary Barcelona in the late 1930s—to what's called "anarchosyndicalism." [Anarchosyndicalism is a form of libertarian socialism that was practiced briefly in regions of Spain during its revolution and civil war of 1936, until it was destroyed by the simultaneous efforts of the Soviet Union, the Western powers, and the Fascists.] I think that's about as high a level as humans have yet achieved in trying to realize these libertarian principles, which in my view are the right ones.

I mean, I'm not saying that everything that was done in that revolution was right, but in its general spirit and character, in the idea of developing the kind of society that Orwell saw and described in I think his greatest work, *Homage to Catalonia*— with popular control over all the institutions of society—okay, that's the right direction in which to move, I think. [. . .]

DEFENDING THE WELFARE STATE

WOMAN: *Noam, since you're an anarchist and often say that you oppose the existence of the nation-state itself and think it's incompatible with true socialism, does that make you at all reluctant to defend welfare programs and other social services which are now under attack from the right wing, and which the right wing wants to dismantle?*

Well, it's true that the anarchist vision in just about all its varieties has looked forward to dismantling state power—and personally I share that vision. But right now it runs directly counter to my goals: my immediate goals have been, and now very much are, to defend and even strengthen certain elements of state authority that are now under severe attack. And I don't think there's any contradiction there—none at all, really.

For example, take the so-called welfare state. What's called the "welfare state" is essentially a recognition that every child has a right to have food, and to have health care and so on—and as I've been saying, those programs were set up in the nation-state system after a century of very hard struggle, by the labor movement, and the socialist movement, and so on. Well, according to the new spirit of the age, in the case of a fourteen-year-old girl who got raped and has a child, her child has to learn "personal responsibility" by not accepting state welfare handouts, meaning, by not having enough to eat. Alright, I don't agree with that at any level. In fact, I think it's grotesque at any level. I think those children should be saved. And in today's world, that's going to have to involve working through the state system; it's not the only case.

So despite the anarchist "vision," I think aspects of the state system, like the one that makes sure children eat, have to be defended—in fact, defended very vigorously. And given the accelerating effort that's being made these days to roll back the victories for justice and human rights which have been won through long and often extremely bitter struggles in the West, in my opinion the immediate goal of even committed anarchists should be to defend some state institutions, while helping to pry them open to more meaningful public participation, and ultimately to dismantle them in a much more free society.

There are practical problems of tomorrow on which people's lives very much depend, and while defending these kinds of programs is by no means the ultimate end we should be pursuing, in my view we still have to face the problems that are right on the horizon, and which seriously affect human lives. I don't think those things can simply be forgotten because they might not fit within some radical slogan that reflects a deeper vision of a future society. The deeper visions should be maintained, they're important—but dismantling the state system is a goal that's a lot farther away, and you want to deal first with what's at hand and nearby, I think. And in any realistic perspective, the political system, with all its flaws, does have opportunities for participation by the general population which other existing institutions, such as corporations, don't have. In fact, that's exactly why the far right wants to *weaken* governmental structures—because if you can make sure that all the key decisions are in the hands of Microsoft and General Electric and Raytheon, then you don't have to worry anymore about the threat of popular involvement in policy-making.

So take something that's been happening in recent years: devolution—that is, removing authority from the federal government down to the state governments. Well, in some circumstances, that would be a democratizing move which I would be in favor of—it would be a move away from central authority down to local authority. But that's in abstract circumstances that don't exist. Right now it'll happen because moving decision-making power down to the state level in fact means handing it over to private power. See, huge corporations can influence and dominate the federal government, but even middle-sized corporations can influence state governments and play one state's workforce off against another's by threatening to move production elsewhere unless they get better tax breaks and so on. So under the conditions of existing systems of power, devolution is very antidemocratic; under other systems of much greater equality, devolution could be highly democratic—but these are questions which really can't be discussed in isolation from the society as it actually exists.

So I think that it's completely realistic and rational to work within structures to which you are opposed, because by doing so you can help to move to a situation where then you can challenge those structures.

Let me just give you an analogy. I don't like to have armed police everywhere, I think it's a bad idea. On the other hand, a number of years ago when I had little kids, there was a rabid raccoon running around our neighborhood biting children.

Well, we tried various ways of getting rid of it—you know, "Have-a-Heart" animal traps, all this kind of stuff—but nothing worked. So finally we just called the police and had them do it: it was better than having the kids bitten by a rabid raccoon, right? Is there a contradiction there? No: in particular circumstances, you sometimes have to accept and use illegitimate structures.

Well, we happen to have a huge rabid raccoon running around—it's called corporations. And there is nothing in the society right now that can protect people from that tyranny, except the federal government. Now, it doesn't protect them very *well*, because mostly it's run by the corporations, but still it does have some limited effect—it can enforce regulatory measures under public pressure, let's say, it can reduce dangerous toxic waste disposal, it can set minimal standards on health care, and so on. In fact, it has various things that it can do to improve the situation when there's this huge rabid raccoon dominating the place. So, fine, I think we ought to get it to do the things it can do—if you can get rid of the *raccoon*, great, then let's dismantle the federal government. But to say, "Okay, let's just get rid of the federal government as soon as we possibly can," and then let the private tyrannies take over *everything*—I mean, for an anarchist to advocate that is just outlandish, in my opinion. So I really don't see any contradiction at all here.

Supporting these aspects of the governmental structures just seems to me to be part of a willingness to face some of the complexities of life for what they are—and the complexities of life include the fact that there are a lot of ugly things out there, and if you care about the fact that some kid in downtown Boston is starving, or that some poor person can't get adequate medical care, or that somebody's going to pour toxic waste in your backyard, or anything at all like that, well, then you try to stop it. And there's only one institution around right now that can stop it. If you just want to be pure and say, "I'm against power, period," well, okay, say, "I'm against the federal government." But that's just to divorce yourself from any human concerns, in my view. And I don't think that's a reasonable stance for anarchists or anyone else to take.

3

Part II of *Objectivity and Liberal Scholarship*

If it is plausible that ideology will in general serve as a mask for self-interest, then it is a natural presumption that intellectuals, in interpreting history or formulating policy, will tend to adopt an elitist position, condemning popular movements and mass participation in decision making, and emphasizing rather the necessity for supervision by those who possess the knowledge and understanding that is required (so they claim) to manage society and control social change. This is hardly a novel thought. One major element in the anarchist critique of Marxism a century ago was the prediction that, as Bakunin formulated it:

According to the theory of Mr. Marx, the people not only must not destroy [the state] but must strengthen it and place it at the complete disposal of their benefactors, guardians, and teachers—the leaders of the Communist party, namely Mr. Marx and his friends, who will proceed to liberate [mankind] in their own way. They will concentrate the reins of government in a strong hand, because the ignorant people require an exceedingly firm guardianship; they will establish a single state bank, concentrating in its hands all commercial, industrial, agricultural and even scientific production, and then divide the masses into two armies—industrial and agricultural—under the direct command of the state engineers, who will constitute a new privileged scientific-political estate.[1]

One cannot fail to be struck by the parallel between this prediction and that of Daniel Bell—the prediction that in the new postindustrial society, "not only the best talents, but eventually the entire complex of social prestige and social status, will be rooted in the intellectual and scientific communities."[2] Pursuing the parallel for a moment, it might be asked whether the left-wing critique of Leninist elitism can be applied, under very different conditions, to the liberal ideology of the intellectual elite that aspires to a dominant role in managing the welfare state.

Rosa Luxemburg, in 1918, argued that Bolshevik elitism would lead to a state of society in which the bureaucracy alone would remain an active element in social life—though now it would be the "red bureaucracy" of that State Socialism that Bakunin had long before described as "the most vile and terrible lie that our century has created."[3] A true social revolution requires a "spiritual transformation in the masses degraded by centuries of bourgeois class rule";[4] "it is only by extirpating the habits of obedience and servility to the last root that the working class can acquire the understanding of a new form of discipline, self-discipline arising from free consent."[5] Writing in 1904, she predicted that Lenin's organizational concepts would "enslave a young labor movement to an intellectual elite hungry for power . . . and turn it into an automaton manipulated by a Central Committee."[6] In the Bolshevik elitist doctrine of 1918 she saw a disparagement of the creative, spontaneous, self-correcting force of mass action, which alone, she argued, could solve the thousand problems of social reconstruction and produce the spiritual transformation that is the essence of a true social revolution. As Bolshevik practice hardened into dogma, the fear of popular initiative and spontaneous mass action, not under the direction and control of the properly designated vanguard, became a dominant element of so-called "Communist" ideology.

Antagonism to mass movements and to social change that escapes the control of privileged elites is also a prominent feature of contemporary liberal ideology.[7] Expressed as foreign policy, it takes the form described earlier. To conclude this discussion of counterrevolutionary subordination, I would like to investigate how, in one rather crucial case, this particular bias in American liberal ideology can be detected even in the interpretation of events of the past in which American involvement was rather slight, and in historical work of very high caliber.

In 1966, the American Historical Association gave its biennial award for the most outstanding work on European history to Gabriel Jackson, for his study of Spain in the 1930s.[8] There is no question that of the dozens of books on this period, Jackson's is among the best, and I do not doubt that the award was well deserved. The Spanish Civil War is one of the crucial events of modern history, and one of the most extensively studied as well. In it, we find the interplay of forces and ideas that have dominated European history since the industrial revolution. What is more, the relationship of Spain to the great powers was in many respects like that of the countries of what is

now called the Third World. In some ways, then, the events of
the Spanish Civil War give a foretaste of what the future may
hold, as Third World revolutions uproot traditional societies,
threaten imperial dominance, exacerbate great-power rivalries,
and bring the world perilously close to a war which, if not
averted, will surely be the final catastrophe of modern history.
My reason for wanting to investigate an outstanding liberal
analysis of the Spanish Civil War is therefore twofold: first, because of the intrinsic interest of these events; and second, because of the insight that this analysis may provide with respect
to the underlying elitist bias which I believe to be at the root of
the phenomenon of counterrevolutionary subordination.

In his study of the Spanish Republic, Jackson makes no
attempt to hide his own commitment in favor of liberal democracy, as represented by such figures as Azaña, Casares
Quiroga, Martínez Barrio,[9] and the other "responsible national
leaders." In taking this position, he speaks for much of liberal
scholarship; it is fair to say that figures similar to those just
mentioned would be supported by American liberals, were this
possible, in Latin America, Asia, or Africa. Furthermore, Jackson makes little attempt to disguise his antipathy towards the
forces of popular revolution in Spain, or their goals.

It is no criticism of Jackson's study that his point of view and
sympathies are expressed with such clarity. On the contrary,
the value of this work as an interpretation of historical events is
enhanced by the fact that the author's commitments are made
so clear and explicit. But I think it can be shown that Jackson's
account of the popular revolution that took place in Spain is
misleading and in part quite unfair, and that the failure of objectivity it reveals is highly significant in that it is characteristic
of the attitude taken by liberal (and Communist) intellectuals

towards revolutionary movements that are largely spontaneous and only loosely organized, while rooted in deeply felt needs and ideals of dispossessed masses. It is a convention of scholarship that the use of such terms as those of the preceding phrase demonstrates naïveté and muddle-headed sentimentality. The convention, however, is supported by ideological conviction rather than history or investigation of the phenomena of social life. This conviction is, I think, belied by such events as the revolution that swept over much of Spain in the summer of 1936.

The circumstances of Spain in the 1930s are not duplicated elsewhere in the underdeveloped world today, to be sure. Nevertheless, the limited information that we have about popular movements in Asia, specifically, suggests certain similar features that deserve much more serious and sympathetic study than they have so far received.[10] Inadequate information makes it hazardous to try to develop any such parallel, but I think it is quite possible to note long-standing tendencies in the response of liberal as well as Communist intellectuals to such mass movements.

As I have already remarked, the Spanish Civil War is not only one of the critical events of modern history but one of the most intensively studied as well. Yet there are surprising gaps. During the months following the Franco insurrection in July 1936, a social revolution of unprecedented scope took place throughout much of Spain. It had no "revolutionary vanguard" and appears to have been largely spontaneous, involving masses of urban and rural laborers in a radical transformation of social and economic conditions that persisted, with remarkable success, until it was crushed by force. This predominantly anarchist revolution and the massive social transformation to which it gave rise are treated, in recent historical studies, as a kind of aberration, a nuisance that stood in the way of successful prosecution of the war to save the bourgeois regime from the Franco rebellion. Many historians would probably agree with Eric Hobsbawm[11] that the *failure* of social revolution in Spain "was due to the anarchists," that anarchism was "a disaster," a kind of "moral gymnastics" with no "concrete results," at best "a profoundly moving spectacle for the student of popular religion." The most extensive historical study of the anarchist revolution[12] is relatively inaccessible, and neither its author, now living in southern France, nor the many refugees who will never write memoirs but who might provide invaluable personal testimony have been consulted, apparently, by writers of the major historical works.[13] The one published collection of documents dealing with collectivization[14] has been published only by an anarchist press and hence is barely accessible to the general reader, and has also rarely been consulted—it does not, for example, appear in Jackson's bibliography, though Jackson's account is intended to be a social and political, not merely a military, history. In fact, this astonishing social upheaval seems to have largely passed from memory. The drama and pathos of the Spanish Civil War have by no means faded; witness the impact a few years ago of the film *To Die in Madrid*. Yet in this film (as Daniel Guérin points out) one finds no reference to the popular revolution that had transformed much of Spanish society.

I will be concerned here with the events of 1936–1937,[15] and with one particular aspect of the complex struggle involving Franco Nationalists, Republicans (including the Communist party), anarchists, and socialist workers' groups. The Franco insurrection in July 1936 came against a background of several months of strikes, expropriations, and battles between peasants and Civil Guards. The left-wing Socialist leader Largo Caballero had demanded in June that the workers be armed, but was refused by Azaña. When the coup came, the Republican government was paralyzed. Workers armed themselves in Madrid and Barcelona, robbing government armories and even ships in the harbor, and put down the insurrection while the government vacillated, torn between the twin dangers of submitting to Franco and arming the working classes. In large areas of Spain effective authority passed into the hands of the anarchist and socialist workers who had played a substantial, generally dominant role in putting down the insurrection.

The next few months have frequently been described as a period of "dual power." In Barcelona industry and commerce were largely collectivized, and a wave of collectivization spread through rural areas, as well as towns and villages, in Aragon, Castile, and the Levant, and to a lesser but still significant extent in many parts of Catalonia, Asturias, Estremadura, and Andalusia. Military power was exercised by defense committees; social and economic organization took many forms, following in main outlines the program of the Saragossa Congress of the anarchist CNT in May 1936. The revolution was "apolitical," in the sense that its organs of power and administration remained separate from the central Republican government and, even after several anarchist leaders entered the government in the autumn of 1936, continued to function fairly independently until the revolution was finally crushed between the fascist and Communist-led Republican forces. The success of collectivization of industry and commerce in Barcelona impressed even highly unsympathetic observers such as Borkenau. The scale of rural collectivization is indicated by these data from anarchist sources: in Aragon, 450 collectives with half a million members; in the Levant, 900 collectives accounting for about half the agricultural production and 70 percent of marketing in this, the richest agricultural region of Spain; in Castile, 300 collectives with about 100,000 members.[16] In Catalonia, the bourgeois government headed by Companys retained nominal authority, but real power was in the hands of the anarchist-dominated committees.

The period of July through September may be characterized as one of spontaneous, widespread, but unconsummated social revolution.[17] A number of anarchist leaders joined the government; the reason, as stated by Federica Montseny on January 3, 1937, was this: ". . . the anarchists have entered the government to prevent the Revolution from deviating and in order to carry it further beyond the war, and also to oppose any dictatorial tendency, from wherever it might come."[18] The central government fell increasingly under Communist control—in Catalonia, under the control of the Communist-dominated PSUC—largely as a result of the valuable Russian military assistance. Communist success was greatest in the rich farming areas of the Levant (the government moved to Valencia, capital of one of the provinces), where prosperous farm owners flocked to the Peasant Federation that the party had organized to protect the wealthy farmers; this federation "served as a powerful instrument in checking the rural collectivization promoted by the agricultural workers of the province."[19] Elsewhere as well, counterrevolutionary successes reflected increasing Communist dominance of the Republic.

The first phase of the counterrevolution was the legalization and regulation of those accomplishments of the revolution that appeared irreversible. A decree of October 7 by the Communist Minister of Agriculture, Vicente Uribe, legalized certain expropriations—namely, of lands belonging to participants in the Franco revolt. Of course, these expropriations had already taken place, a fact that did not prevent the Communist press from describing the decree as "the most profoundly revolutionary measure that has been taken since the military uprising."[20] In fact, by exempting the estates of landowners who had not directly participated in the Franco rebellion, the decree represented a step backward, from the standpoint of the revolutionaries, and it was criticized not only by the CNT but also by the Socialist Federation of Land Workers, affiliated with the UGT. The demand for a much broader decree was unacceptable to the Communist-led ministry, since the Communist party was "seeking support among the propertied classes in the anti-Franco coup" and hence "could not afford to repel the small and medium proprietors who had been hostile to the working class movement before the civil war."[21] These "small proprietors," in fact, seem to have included owners of substantial estates. The decree compelled tenants to continue paying rent unless the landowners had supported Franco, and by guaranteeing former landholdings, it prevented distribution of land to the village poor. Ricardo Zabalza, general secretary of the Federation of Land Workers, described the resulting situation as one of "galling injustice"; "the sycophants of the former political bosses still enjoy a privileged position at the expense of those persons who were unable to rent even the smallest parcel of land, because they were revolutionaries."[22]

To complete the stage of legalization and restriction of what had already been achieved, a decree of October 24, 1936, promulgated by a CNT member who had become Councilor for

Economy in the Catalonian Generalitat, gave legal sanction to the collectivization of industry in Catalonia. In this case too, the step was regressive, from the revolutionary point of view. Collectivization was limited to enterprises employing more than a hundred workers, and a variety of conditions were established that removed control from the workers' committees to the state bureaucracy.[23]

The second stage of the counterrevolution, from October 1936 through May 1937, involved the destruction of the local committees, the replacement of the militia by a conventional army, and the re-establishment of the prerevolutionary social and economic system, wherever this was possible. Finally, in May 1937, came a direct attack on the working class in Barcelona (the May Days).[24] Following the success of this attack, the process of liquidation of the revolution was completed. The collectivization decree of October 24 was rescinded and industries were "freed" from workers' control. Communist-led armies swept through Aragon, destroying many collectives and dismantling their organizations and, generally, bringing the area under the control of the central government. Throughout the Republican-held territories, the government, now under Communist domination, acted in accordance with the plan announced in *Pravda* on December 17, 1936: "So far as Catalonia is concerned, the cleaning up of Trotzkyist and Anarcho-Syndicalist elements there has already begun, and it will be carried out there with the same energy as in the U.S.S.R."[25] — and, we may add, in much the same manner.

In brief, the period from the summer of 1936 to 1937 was one of revolution and counterrevolution: the revolution was largely spontaneous with mass participation of anarchist and socialist industrial and agricultural workers; the counterrevolution was under Communist direction, the Communist party increasingly coming to represent the right wing of the Republic. During this period and after the success of the counterrevolution, the Republic was waging a war against the Franco insurrection; this has been described in great detail in numerous publications, and I will say little about it here. The Communist-led counterrevolutionary struggle must, of course, be understood against the background of the ongoing antifascist war and the more general attempt of the Soviet Union to construct a broad antifascist alliance with the Western democracies. One reason for the vigorous counterrevolutionary policy of the Communists was their belief that England would never tolerate a revolutionary triumph in Spain, where England had substantial commercial interests, as did France and to a lesser extent the United States.[26] I will return to this matter below. However, I think it is important to bear in mind that there were undoubtedly other factors as well. Rudolf Rocker's comments are, I believe, quite to the point:

> . . . the Spanish people have been engaged in a desperate struggle against a pitiless foe and have been exposed besides to the secret intrigues of the great imperialist powers of Europe. Despite this the Spanish revolutionaries have not grasped at the disastrous expedient of dictatorship, but have respected all honest convictions. Everyone who visited Barcelona after the July battles, whether friend or foe of the C.N.T., was surprised at the freedom of public life and the absence of any arrangements for suppressing the free expression of opinion.
>
> For two decades the supporters of Bolshevism have been hammering it into the masses that dictatorship is a vital necessity for the defense of the so-called proletarian interests against

the assaults of the counter-revolution and for paving the way for Socialism. They have not advanced the cause of Socialism by this propaganda, but have merely smoothed the way for Fascism in Italy, Germany and Austria by causing millions of people to forget that dictatorship, the most extreme form of tyranny, can never lead to social liberation. In Russia, the so-called dictatorship of the proletariat has not led to Socialism, but to the domination of a new bureaucracy over the proletariat and the whole people. . . .

What the Russian autocrats and their supporters fear most is that the success of libertarian Socialism in Spain might prove to their blind followers that the much vaunted "necessity of a dictatorship" is nothing but one vast fraud which in Russia has led to the despotism of Stalin and is to serve today in Spain to help the counter-revolution to a victory over the revolution of the workers and peasants.[27]

After decades of anti-Communist indoctrination, it is difficult to achieve a perspective that makes possible a serious evaluation of the extent to which Bolshevism and Western liberalism have been united in their opposition to popular revolution. However, I do not think that one can comprehend the events in Spain without attaining this perspective.

With this brief sketch—partisan, but I think accurate—for background, I would like to turn to Jackson's account of this aspect of the Spanish Civil War (see note 8).

Jackson presumes (p. 259) that Soviet support for the Republican cause in Spain was guided by two factors: first, concern for Soviet security; second, the hope that a Republican victory would advance "the cause of worldwide 'people's revolution' with which Soviet leaders hoped to identify themselves." They did not press their revolutionary aims, he feels, because "for the moment it was essential not to frighten the middle classes or the Western governments."

As to the concern for Soviet security, Jackson is no doubt correct. It is clear that Soviet support of the Republic was one aspect of the attempt to make common cause with the Western democracies against the fascist threat. However, Jackson's conception of the Soviet Union as a revolutionary power—hopeful that a Republican victory would advance "the interrupted movement toward world revolution" and seeking to identify itself with "the cause of the world-wide 'people's revolution' "—seems to me entirely mistaken. Jackson presents no evidence to support this interpretation of Soviet policy, nor do I know of any. It is interesting to see how differently the events were interpreted at the time of the Spanish Civil War, not only by anarchists like Rocker but also by such commentators as Gerald Brenan and Franz Borkenau, who were intimately acquainted with the situation in Spain. Brenan observes that the counter-revolutionary policy of the Communists (which he thinks was "extremely sensible") was

> the policy most suited to the Communists themselves. Russia is a totalitarian regime ruled by a bureaucracy: the frame of mind of its leaders, who have come through the most terrible upheaval in history, is cynical and opportunist: the whole fabric of the state is dogmatic and authoritarian. To expect such men to lead a social revolution in a country like Spain, where the wildest idealism is combined with great independence of character, was out of the question. The Russians could, it is true, command plenty of idealism among their foreign admirers, but they could only harness it to the creation of a cast-iron

bureaucratic state, where everyone thinks alike and obeys the orders of the chief above him.[28]

He sees nothing in Russian conduct in Spain to indicate any interest in a "people's revolution." Rather, the Communist policy was to oppose "even such rural and industrial collectives as had risen spontaneously and flood the country with police who, like the Russian Ogpu, acted on the orders of their party rather than those of the Ministry of the Interior." The Communists were concerned to suppress altogether the impulses towards "spontaneity of speech or action," since "their whole nature and history made them distrust the local and spontaneous and put their faith in order, discipline and bureaucratic uniformity"—hence placed them in opposition to the revolutionary forces in Spain. As Brenan also notes, the Russians withdrew their support once it became clear that the British would not be swayed from the policy of appeasement, a fact which gives additional confirmation to the thesis that only considerations of Russian foreign policy led the Soviet Union to support the Republic.

Borkenau's analysis is similar. He approves of the Communist policy, because of its "efficiency," but he points out that the Communists "put an end to revolutionary social activity, and enforced their view that this ought not to be a revolution but simply the defence of a legal government . . . communist policy in Spain was mainly dictated not by the necessities of the Spanish fight but by the interests of the intervening foreign power, Russia," a country "with a revolutionary past, not a revolutionary present." The Communists acted "not with the aim of transforming chaotic enthusiasm into disciplined enthusiasm [which Borkenau feels to have been necessary], but with the aim of substituting disciplined military and administrative action for the action of the masses and getting rid of the latter entirely." This policy, he points out, went "directly against the interests and claims of the masses" and thus weakened popular support. The now apathetic masses would not commit themselves to the defense of a Communist-run dictatorship, which restored former authority and even "showed a definite preference for the police forces of the old regime, so hated by the masses." It seems to me that the record strongly supports this interpretation of Communist policy and its effects, though Borkenau's assumption that Communist "efficiency" was necessary to win the anti-Franco struggle is much more dubious— a question to which I return below.[29]

It is relevant to observe, at this point, that a number of the Spanish Communist leaders were reluctantly forced to similar conclusions. Bolloten cites several examples,[30] specifically, the military commander "El Campesino" and Jesús Hernández, a minister in the Caballero government. The former, after his escape from the Soviet Union in 1949, stated that he had taken for granted the "revolutionary solidarity" of the Soviet Union during the Civil War—a most remarkable degree of innocence—and realized only later "that the Kremlin does not serve the interests of the peoples of the world, but makes them serve its own interests; that, with a treachery and hypocrisy without parallel, it makes use of the international working class as a mere pawn in its political intrigues." Hernández, in a speech given shortly after the Civil War, admits that the Spanish Communist leaders "acted more like Soviet subjects than sons of the Spanish people." "It may seem absurd, incredible," he adds, "but our education under Soviet tutelage had deformed us to such an extent that we were completely

denationalized; our national soul was torn out of us and replaced by a rabidly chauvinistic internationalism, which began
and ended with the towers of the Kremlin."

Shortly after the Third World Congress of the Communist International in 1921, the Dutch "ultra-leftist" Hermann
Gorter wrote that the congress "has decided the fate of the
world revolution for the present. The trend of opinion that seriously desired world revolution . . . has been expelled from the
Russian International. The Communist Parties in western Europe and throughout the world that retain their membership
of the Russian International will become nothing more than
a means to preserve the Russian Revolution and the Soviet
Republic."[31] This forecast has proved quite accurate. Jackson's
conception that the Soviet Union was a revolutionary power
in the late 1930s, or even that the Soviet leaders truly regarded
themselves as identified with world revolution, is without factual support. It is a misinterpretation that runs parallel to the
American Cold War mythology that has invented an "international Communist conspiracy" directed from Moscow (now
Peking) to justify its own interventionist policies.

Turning to events in revolutionary Spain, Jackson describes
the first stages of collectivization as follows: the unions in
Madrid, "as in Barcelona and Valencia, abused their sudden
authority to place the sign *incautado* [placed under workers'
control] on all manner of buildings and vehicles" (p. 279).
Why was this an *abuse* of authority? This Jackson does not explain. The choice of words indicates a reluctance on Jackson's
part to recognize the reality of the revolutionary situation,
despite his account of the breakdown of Republican authority.
The statement that the workers "abused their sudden authority" by carrying out collectivization rests on a moral judgment

that recalls that of Ithiel Pool, when he characterizes land reform in Vietnam as a matter of "despoiling one's neighbors," or of Franz Borkenau, when he speaks of expropriation in the Soviet Union as "robbery," demonstrating "a streak of moral indifference."

Within a few months, Jackson informs us, "the revolutionary tide began to ebb in Catalonia" after "accumulating food and supply problems, and the experience of administering villages, frontier posts, and public utilities, had rapidly shown the anarchists the unsuspected complexity of modern society" (pp. 313–14). In Barcelona, "the naïve optimism of the revolutionary conquests of the previous August had given way to feelings of resentment and of somehow having been cheated," as the cost of living doubled, bread was in short supply, and police brutality reached the levels of the monarchy. "The POUM and the anarchist press simultaneously extolled the collectivizations and explained the failures of production as due to Valencia policies of boycotting the Catalan economy and favoring the *bourgeoisie*. They explained the loss of Málaga as due in large measure to the low morale and the disorientation of the Andalusian proletariat, which saw the Valencia government evolving steadily toward the right" (p. 368). Jackson evidently believes that this left-wing interpretation of events was nonsensical, and that in fact it was anarchist incompetence or treachery that was responsible for the difficulties: "In Catalonia, the CNT factory committees dragged their heels on war production, claiming that the government deprived them of raw materials and was favoring the *bourgeoisie*" (p. 365).

In fact, "the revolutionary tide began to ebb in Catalonia" under a middle-class attack led by the Communist party, not because of a recognition of the "complexity of modern society." And it was, moreover, quite true that the Communist-dominated central government attempted, with much success, to hamper collectivized industry and agriculture and to disrupt the collectivization of commerce. I have already referred to the early stages of counterrevolution. Further investigation of the sources to which Jackson refers and others shows that the anarchist charges were not baseless, as Jackson implies. Bolloten cites a good deal of evidence in support of his conclusion that

> In the countryside the Communists undertook a spirited defence of the small and medium proprietor and tenant farmer against the collectivizing drive of the rural wage-workers, against the policy of the labour unions prohibiting the farmer from holding more land than he could cultivate with his own hands, and against the practices of revolutionary committees, which requisitioned harvests, interfered with private trade, and collected rents from tenant farmers.[32]

The policy of the government was clearly enunciated by the Communist Minister of Agriculture: "We say that the property of the small farmer is sacred and that those who attack or attempt to attack this property must be regarded as enemies of the regime."[33] Gerald Brenan, no sympathizer with collectivization, explains the failure of collectivization as follows (p. 321):

> The Central Government, and especially the Communist and Socialist members of it, desired to bring [the collectives] under the direct control of the State: they therefore failed to provide them with the credit required for buying raw materials: as soon as the supply of raw cotton was exhausted the

mills stopped working . . . even [the munitions industry in Catalonia] were harassed by the new bureaucratic organs of the Ministry of Supply.[34]

He quotes the bourgeois president of Catalonia, Companys, as saying that "workers in the arms factories in Barcelona had been working 56 hours and more each week and that no cases of sabotage or indiscipline had taken place," until the workers were demoralized by the bureaucratization—later, militarization—imposed by the central government and the Communist party.[35] His own conclusion is that "the Valencia Government was now using the P.S.U.C. against the C.N.T.— but not . . . because the Catalan workers were giving trouble, but because the Communists wished to weaken them before destroying them."

The cited correspondence from Companys to Prieto, according to Vernon Richards (p. 47), presents evidence showing the success of Catalonian war industry under collectivization and demonstrating how "much more could have been achieved had the means for expanding the industry not been denied them by the Central Government." Richards also cites testimony by a spokesman for the subsecretariat of munitions and armament of the Valencia government admitting that "the war industry of Catalonia had produced ten times more than the rest of Spanish industry put together and [agreeing] . . . that this output could have been quadrupled as from beginning of September* if Catalonia had had access to the necessary means for purchasing raw materials that were

---

* The quoted testimony is from September 1, 1937; presumably, the reference is to September 1936.

unobtainable in Spanish territory." It is important to recall that
the central government had enormous gold reserves (soon to
be transmitted to the Soviet Union), so that raw materials for
Catalan industry could probably have been purchased, despite
the hostility of the Western democracies to the Republic during the revolutionary period (see below). Furthermore, raw
materials had repeatedly been requested. On September 24,
1936, Juan Fabregas, the CNT delegate to the Economic
Council of Catalonia who was in part responsible for the collectivization decree cited earlier, reported that the financial
difficulties of Catalonia were created by the refusal of the
central government to "give any assistance in economic and
financial questions, presumably because it has little sympathy
with the work of a practical order which is being carried out in
Catalonia"[36]—that is, collectivization. He "went on to recount
that a Commission which went to Madrid to ask for credits to
purchase war materials and raw materials, offering 1,000 million pesetas in securities lodged in the Bank of Spain, met
with a blank refusal. It was sufficient that the new war industry
in Catalonia was controlled by the workers of the C.N.T. for
the Madrid Government to refuse any unconditional aid. Only
in exchange for government control would they give financial
assistance."[37]

Broué and Témime take a rather similar position. Commenting on the charge of "incompetence" leveled against
the collectivized industries, they point out that "one must not
neglect the terrible burden of the war." Despite this burden,
they observe, "new techniques of management and elimina-
tion of dividends had permitted a lowering of prices" and
"mechanisation and rationalization, introduced in numerous
enterprises . . . had considerably augmented production. The

workers accepted the enormous sacrifices with enthusiasm because, in most cases, they had the conviction that the factory belonged to them and that at last they were working for themselves and their class brothers. A truly new spirit had come over the economy of Spain with the concentration of scattered enterprises, the simplification of commercial patterns, a significant structure of social projects for aged workers, children, disabled, sick and the personnel in general" (pp. 150–51). The great weakness of the revolution, they argue, was the fact that it was not carried through to completion. In part this was because of the war; in part, a consequence of the policies of the central government. They too emphasize the refusal of the Madrid government, in the early stages of collectivization, to grant credits or supply funds to collectivized industry or agriculture—in the case of Catalonia, even when substantial guarantees were offered by the Catalonian government. Thus the collectivized enterprises were forced to exist on what assets had been seized at the time of the revolution. The control of gold and credit "permitted the government to restrict and prevent the function of collective enterprises at will" (p. 144).

According to Broué and Témime, it was the restriction of credit that finally destroyed collectivized industry. The Companys government in Catalonia refused to create a bank for industry and credit, as demanded by the CNT and POUM, and the central government (relying, in this case, on control of the banks by the socialist UGT) was able to control the flow of capital and "to reserve credit for private enterprise." All attempts to obtain credit for collectivized industry were unsuccessful, they maintain, and "the movement of collectivization was restricted, then halted, the government remaining in control of industry through the medium of the banks . . .

[and later] through its control of the choice of managers and directors," who often turned out to be the former owners and managers, under new titles. The situation was similar in the case of collectivized agriculture (pp. 204f).

The situation was duly recognized in the West. The *New York Times*, in February 1938, observed: "The principle of State intervention and control of business and industry, as against workers' control of them in the guise of collectivization, is gradually being established in loyalist Spain by a series of decrees now appearing. Coincidentally there is to be established the principle of private ownership and the rights of corporations and companies to what is lawfully theirs under the Constitution." [38]

Morrow cites (pp. 64–65) a series of acts by the Catalonian government restricting collectivization, once power had shifted away from the new institutions set up by the workers' revolution of July 1936. On February 3, the collectivization of the dairy trade was declared illegal. [39] In April, "the Generalidad annulled workers' control over the customs by refusing to certify workers' ownership of material that had been exported and was being tied up in foreign courts by suits of former owners; henceforth the factories and agricultural collectives exporting goods were at the mercy of the government." In May, as has already been noted, the collectivization decree of October 24 was rescinded, with the argument that the decree "was dictated without competency by the Generalidad," because "there was not, nor is there yet, legislation of the [Spanish] state to apply" and "article 44 of the Constitution declares expropriation and socialization are functions of the State." A decree of August 28 "gave the government the right to intervene in or take over any mining or metallurgical plant." The anarchist newspaper *Solidaridad Obrera* reported in October a decision of the department of purchases of the Ministry of Defense that it would make contracts for purchases only with enterprises functioning "on the basis of their old owners" or "under the corresponding intervention controlled by the Ministry of Finance and Economy."[40]

Returning to Jackson's statement that "In Catalonia, the CNT factory committees dragged their heels on war production, claiming that the government deprived them of raw materials and was favoring the *bourgeoisie*," I believe one must conclude that this statement is more an expression of Jackson's bias in favor of capitalist democracy than a description of the historical facts. At the very least, we can say this much: Jackson presents no evidence to support his conclusion; there is a factual basis for questioning it. I have cited a number of sources that the liberal historian would regard, quite correctly, as biased in favor of the revolution. My point is that the failure of objectivity, the deepseated bias of liberal historians, is a matter much less normally taken for granted, and that there are good grounds for supposing that this failure of objectivity has seriously distorted the judgments that are rather brashly handed down about the nature of the Spanish revolution.

Continuing with the analysis of Jackson's judgments, unsupported by any cited evidence, consider his remark, quoted above, that in Barcelona "the naïve optimism of the revolutionary conquests of the previous August had given way to feelings of resentment and of somehow having been cheated." It is a fact that by January 1937 there was great disaffection in Barcelona. But was this simply a consequence of "the unsuspected complexity of modern society"? Looking into the matter a bit more closely, we see a rather different picture. Under

Russian pressure, the PSUC was given substantial control of the Catalonian government, "putting into the Food Ministry [in December 1936] the man most to the Right in present Catalan politics, Comorera"[41]—by virtue of his political views, the most willing collaborator with the general Communist party position. According to Jackson, Comorera "immediately took steps to end barter and requisitioning, and became a defender of the peasants against the revolution" (p. 314); he "ended requisition, restored money payments, and protected the Catalan peasants against further collectivization" (p. 361). This is all that Jackson has to say about Juan Comorera.

We learn more from other sources: for example, Borkenau, who was in Barcelona for the second time in January 1937—and is universally recognized as a highly knowledgeable and expert observer, with strong anti-anarchist sentiments. According to Borkenau, Comorera represented "a political attitude which can best be compared with that of the extreme right wing of the German social-democracy. He had always regarded the fight against anarchism as the chief aim of socialist policy in Spain. . . . To his surprise, he found unexpected allies for his dislike [of anarchist policies] in the communists."[42] It was impossible to reverse collectivization of industry at that stage in the process of counterrevolution; Comorera did succeed, however, in abolishing the system by which the provisioning of Barcelona had been organized, namely, the village committees, mostly under CNT influence, which had cooperated (perhaps, Borkenau suggests, unwillingly) in delivering flour to the towns. Continuing, Borkenau describes the situation as follows:

. . . Comorera, starting from those principles of abstract liberalism which no administration has followed during the war, but of which right-wing socialists are the last and most religious admirers, did not substitute for the chaotic bread committees a centralized administration. He restored private commerce in bread, simply and completely. There was, in January, not even a system of rationing in Barcelona. Workers were simply left to get their bread, with wages which had hardly changed since May, at increased prices, as well as they could. In practice it meant that the women had to form queues from four o'clock in the morning onwards. The resentment in the working-class districts was naturally acute, the more so as the scarcity of bread rapidly increased after Comorera had taken office.[43]

In short, the workers of Barcelona were not merely giving way to "feelings of resentment and of somehow having been cheated" when they learned of "the unsuspected complexity of modern society." Rather, they had good reason to believe that they *were* being cheated, by the old dog with the new collar.

George Orwell's observations are also highly relevant:

Everyone who has made two visits, at intervals of months, to Barcelona during the war has remarked upon the extraordinary changes that took place in it. And curiously enough, whether they went there first in August and again in January, or, like myself, first in December and again in April, the thing they said was always the same: that the revolutionary atmosphere had vanished. No doubt to anyone who had been there in August, when the blood was scarcely dry in the streets and militia were quartered in the small hotels, Barcelona in December would have seemed bourgeois; to me, fresh from England, it was liker to a workers' city than anything

I had conceived possible. Now [in April] the tide had rolled
back. Once again it was an ordinary city, a little pinched
and chipped by war, but with no outward sign of working-
class predominance. . . . Fat prosperous men, elegant women,
and sleek cars were everywhere. . . . The officers of the new
Popular Army, a type that had scarcely existed when I left
Barcelona, swarmed in surprising numbers . . . [wearing] an
elegant khaki uniform with a tight waist, like a British Army
officer's uniform, only a little more so. I do not suppose that
more than one in twenty of them had yet been to the front,
but all of them had automatic pistols strapped to their belts;
we, at the front, could not get pistols for love or money. . . .*
A deep change had come over the town. There were two facts
that were the keynote of all else. One was that the people—the
civil population—had lost much of their interest in the war;
the other was that the normal division of society into rich and
poor, upper class and lower class, was reasserting itself.[44]

Whereas Jackson attributes the ebbing of the revolutionary
tide to the discovery of the unsuspected complexity of modern
society, Orwell's firsthand observations, like those of Borkenau, suggest a far simpler explanation. What calls for explanation is not the disaffection of the workers of Barcelona but the
curious constructions of the historian.

Let me repeat, at this point, Jackson's comments regarding
Juan Comorera: Comorera "immediately took steps to end barter and requisitioning, and became a defender of the peasants
against the revolution"; he "ended requisitions, restored money

---

*Orwell had just returned from the Aragon front, where he had been
serving with the POUM militia in an area heavily dominated by left-wing
(POUM and anarchist) troops.

payments, and protected the Catalan peasants against further collectivization." These comments imply that the peasantry of Catalonia was, as a body, opposed to the revolution and that Comorera put a stop to the collectivization that they feared. Jackson nowhere indicates any divisions among the peasantry on this issue and offers no support for the implied claim that collectivization was in process at the period of Comorera's access to power. In fact, it is questionable that Comorera's rise to power affected the course of collectivization in Catalonia. Evidence is difficult to come by, but it seems that collectivization of agriculture in Catalonia was not, in any event, extensive, and that it was not extending in December, when Comorera took office. We know from anarchist sources that there had been instances of forced collectivization in Catalonia,[45] but I can find no evidence that Comorera "protected the peasantry" from forced collectivization. Furthermore, it is misleading, at best, to imply that the peasantry *as a whole* was opposed to collectivization. A more accurate picture is presented by Bolloten (p. 56), who points out that "if the individual farmer viewed with dismay the swift and widespread development of collectivized agriculture, the farm workers of the Anarchosyndicalist CNT and the Socialist UGT saw in it, on the contrary, the commencement of a new era." In short, there was a complex class struggle in the countryside, though one learns little about it from Jackson's oversimplified and misleading account. It would seem fair to suppose that this distortion again reflects Jackson's antipathy towards the revolution and its goals. I will return to this question directly, with reference to areas where agricultural collectivization was much more extensive than in Catalonia.

The complexities of modern society that baffled and

confounded the unsuspecting anarchist workers of Barcelona, as Jackson enumerates them, were the following: the accumulating food and supply problems and the administration of frontier posts, villages, and public utilities. As just noted, the food and supply problems seem to have accumulated most rapidly under the brilliant leadership of Juan Comorera. So far as the frontier posts are concerned, the situation, as Jackson elsewhere describes it (p. 368), was basically as follows: "In Catalonia the anarchists had, ever since July 18, controlled the customs stations at the French border. On April 17, 1937, the reorganized carabineros, acting on orders of the Finance Minister, Juan Negrín, began to reoccupy the frontier. At least eight anarchists were killed in clashes with the carabineros." Apart from this difficulty, admittedly serious, there seems little reason to suppose that the problem of manning frontier posts contributed to the ebbing of the revolutionary tide. The available records do not indicate that the problems of administering villages or public utilities were either "unsuspected" or too complex for the Catalonian workers—a remarkable and unsuspected development, but one which nevertheless appears to be borne out by the evidence available to us. I want to emphasize again that Jackson presents no evidence to support his conclusions about the ebbing of the revolutionary tide and the reasons for the disaffection of the Catalonian workers. Once again, I think it fair to attribute his conclusions to the elitist bias of the liberal intellectual rather than to the historical record.

Consider next Jackson's comment that the anarchists "explained the loss of Málaga as due in large measure to the low morale and the disorientation of the Andalusian proletariat, which saw the Valencia government evolving steadily toward the right." Again, it seems that Jackson regards this as just another indication of the naïveté and unreasonableness of the Spanish anarchists. However, here again there is more to the story. One of the primary sources that Jackson cites is Borkenau, quite naturally, since Borkenau spent several days in the area just prior to the fall of Málaga on February 8, 1937. But Borkenau's detailed observations tend to bear out the anarchist "explanation," at least in part. He believed that Málaga might have been saved, but only by a "fight of despair" with mass involvement, of a sort that "the anarchists might have led." But two factors prevented such a defense: first, the officer assigned to lead the defense, Lieutenant Colonel Villalba, "interpreted this task as a purely military one, whereas in reality he had no military means at his disposal but only the forces of a popular movement"; he was a professional officer, "who in the secrecy of his heart hated the spirit of the militia" and was incapable of comprehending the "political factor."[46] A second factor was the significant decline, by February, of political consciousness and mass involvement. The anarchist committees were no longer functioning and the authority of the police and Civil Guards had been restored. "The nuisance of hundreds of independent village police bodies had disappeared, but with it the passionate interest of the village in the civil war. . . . The short interlude of the Spanish Soviet system was at an end" (p. 212). After reviewing the local situation in Málaga and the conflicts in the Valencia government (which failed to provide support or arms for the militia defending Málaga), Borkenau concludes (p. 228): "The Spanish republic paid with the fall of Málaga for the decision of the Right wing of its camp to make an end of social revolution and of its Left wing not to allow that." Jackson's discussion of the fall of Málaga refers to the terror and political rivalries within the town but makes no reference to the fact that Borkenau's description, and the accompanying interpretation, do support the belief that the defeat was due in large measure to low morale and to the incapacity, or unwillingness, of the Valencia government to fight a popular war. On the contrary, he concludes that Colonel Villalba's lack of means for "controlling the bitter political rivalries" was one factor that prevented him from carrying out the essential military tasks. Thus he seems to adopt the view that Borkenau condemns, that the task was a "purely military one." Borkenau's eyewitness account appears to me much more convincing.

In this case too Jackson has described the situation in a somewhat misleading fashion, perhaps again because of the elitist bias that dominates the liberal-Communist interpretation of the Civil War. Like Lieutenant Colonel Villalba, liberal historians often reveal a strong distaste for "the forces of a popular movement" and "the spirit of the militia." And an argument can be given that they correspondingly fail to comprehend the "political factor."

In the May Days of 1937, the revolution in Catalonia received the final blow. On May 3, the councilor for public order, PSUC member Rodríguez Salas, appeared at the central telephone building with a detachment of police, without prior warning or consultation with the anarchist ministers in the government, to take over the telephone exchange. The exchange, formerly the property of IT&T, had been captured by Barcelona workers in July and had since functioned under the control of a UGT-CNT committee, with a governmental delegate, quite in accord with the collectivization decree of October 24, 1936. According to the London *Daily Worker* (May 11, 1937), "Salas sent the armed republican police to disarm the

employees there, most of them members of the CNT unions."
The motive, according to Juan Comorera, was "to put a stop
to an abnormal situation," namely, that no one could speak
over the telephone "without the indiscreet ear of the control-
ler knowing it."[47] Armed resistance in the telephone building
prevented its occupation. Local defense committees erected
barricades throughout Barcelona. Companys and the anarchist
leaders pleaded with the workers to disarm. An uneasy truce
continued until May 6, when the first detachments of Assault
Guards arrived, violating the promises of the government that
the truce would be observed and military forces withdrawn.
The troops were under the command of General Pozas, formerly commander of the hated Civil Guard and now a member of the Communist party. In the fighting that followed,
there were some five hundred killed and over a thousand
wounded. "The May Days in reality sounded the death-knell
of the revolution, announcing political defeat for all and death
for certain of the revolutionary leaders."[48]

These events—of enormous significance in the history of
the Spanish revolution—Jackson sketches in bare outline as a
marginal incident. Obviously the historian's account must be
selective; from the left-liberal point of view that Jackson shares
with Hugh Thomas and many others, the liquidation of the
revolution in Catalonia was a minor event, as the revolution
itself was merely a kind of irrelevant nuisance, a minor irri-
tant diverting energy from the struggle to save the bourgeois
government. The decision to crush the revolution by force is
described as follows:

On May 5, Companys obtained a fragile truce, on the basis of
which the PSUC councilors were to retire from the regional

government, and the question of the Telephone Company was left to future negotiation. That very night, however, Antonio Sesé, a UGT official who was about to enter the reorganized cabinet, was murdered. In any event, the Valencia authorities were in no mood to temporize further with the Catalan Left. On May 6 several thousand *asaltos* arrived in the city, and the Republican Navy demonstrated in the port.[49]

What is interesting about this description is what is left unsaid. For example, there is no comment on the fact that the dispatch of the *asaltos* violated the "fragile truce" that had been accepted by the Barcelona workers and the anarchist and the POUM troops nearby, and barely a mention of the bloody consequences or the political meaning of this unwillingness "to temporize further with the Catalan Left." There is no mention of the fact that along with Sesé, Berneri and other anarchist leaders were murdered, not only during the May Days but in the weeks preceding.[50] Jackson does not refer to the fact that along with the Republican navy, British ships also "demonstrated" in the port.[51] Nor does he refer to Orwell's telling observations about the Assault Guards, as compared to the troops at the front, where he had spent the preceding months. The Assault Guards "were splendid troops, much the best I had seen in Spain. . . . I was used to the ragged, scarcely-armed militia on the Aragon front, and I had not known that the Republic possessed troops like these. . . . The Civil Guards and Carabineros, who were not intended for the front at all, were better armed and far better clad than ourselves. I suspect it is the same in all wars—always the same contrast between the sleek police in the rear and the ragged soldiers in the line."[52] (See page 80 below.)

The contrast reveals a good deal about the nature of the war, as it was understood by the Valencia government. Later, Orwell was to make this conclusion explicit: "A government which sends boys of fifteen to the front with rifles forty years old and keeps its biggest men and newest weapons in the rear is manifestly more afraid of the revolution than of the fascists. Hence the feeble war policy of the past six months, and hence the compromise with which the war will almost certainly end."[53] Jackson's account of these events, with its omissions and assumptions, suggests that he perhaps shares the view that the greatest danger in Spain would have been a victory of the revolution.

Jackson apparently discounts Orwell's testimony, to some extent, commenting that "the readers should bear in mind Orwell's own honest statement that he knew very little about the political complexities of the struggle." This is a strange comment. For one thing, Orwell's analysis of the "political complexities of the struggle" bears up rather well after thirty years; if it is defective, it is probably in his tendency to give too much prominence to the POUM in comparison with the anarchists—not surprising, in view of the fact that he was with the POUM militia. His exposure of the fatuous nonsense that was appearing at the time in the Stalinist and liberal presses appears quite accurate, and later discoveries have given little reason to challenge the basic facts that he reported or the interpretation that he proposed in the heat of the conflict. Orwell does, in fact, refer to his own "political ignorance." Commenting on the final defeat of the revolution in May, he states: "I realized—though owing to my political ignorance, not so clearly as I ought to have done—that when the Government felt more sure of itself there would be reprisals." But this form of "political ignorance" has simply been compounded in more recent historical work.

Shortly after the May Days, the Caballero government fell and Juan Negrín became premier of Republican Spain. Negrín is described as follows, by Broué and Témime: ". . . he is an unconditional defender of capitalist property and resolute adversary of collectivization, whom the CNT ministers find blocking all of their proposals. He is the one who solidly reorganized the carabineros and presided over the transfer of the gold reserves of the Republic to the USSR. He enjoyed the confidence of the moderates . . . [and] was on excellent terms with the Communists."

The first major act of the Negrín government was the suppression of the POUM and the consolidation of central control over Catalonia. The government next turned to Aragon, which had been under largely anarchist control since the first days of the revolution, and where agricultural collectivization was quite extensive and Communist elements very weak. The municipal councils of Aragon were coordinated by the Council of Aragon, headed by Joaquín Ascaso, a well-known CNT militant, one of whose brothers had been killed during the May Days. Under the Caballero government, the anarchists had agreed to give representation to other antifascist parties, including the Communists, but the majority remained anarchist. In August the Negrín government announced the dissolution of the Council of Aragon and dispatched a division of the Spanish army, commanded by the Communist officer Enrique Lister, to enforce the dissolution of the local committees, dismantle the collectives, and establish central government control. Ascaso was arrested on the charge of having been responsible for the robbery of jewelry—namely, the jewelry "robbed" by the Council for its own use in the fall of 1936. The local anarchist press was suppressed in favor of a Communist journal, and in general local anarchist centers were forcefully occupied and closed. The last anarchist stronghold was captured, with tanks and artillery, on September 21. Because of government-imposed censorship, there is very little of a direct record of these events, and the major histories pass over them quickly.[54] According to Morrow, "the official CNT press . . . compared the assault on Aragon with the subjection of Asturias by Lopez Ochoa in October 1934"—the latter, one of the bloodiest acts of repression in modern Spanish history. Although this is an exaggeration, it is a fact that the popular organs of administration were wiped out by Lister's legions, and the revolution was now over, so far as Aragon was concerned.

About these events, Jackson has the following comments:

> On August 11 the government announced the dissolution of the *Consejo de Aragón*, the anarchist-dominated administration which had been recognized by Largo Caballero in December, 1936. The peasants were known to hate the Consejo, the anarchists had deserted the front during the Barcelona fighting, and the very existence of the Consejo was a standing challenge to the authority of the central government. For all these reasons Negrín did not hesitate to send in troops, and to arrest the anarchist officials. Once their authority had been broken, however, they were released.[55]

These remarks are most interesting. Consider first the charge that the anarchists had deserted the front during the May Days. It is true that elements of certain anarchist and POUM divisions were prepared to march on Barcelona, but after the "fragile truce" was established on May 5, they did not do so; no anarchist forces even approached Barcelona to defend the Barcelona proletariat and its institutions from attack. However, a motorized column of 5,000 Assault Guards was sent from the front by the government to break the "fragile truce."[56] Hence the only forces to "desert the front" during the Barcelona fighting were those dispatched by the government to complete the job of dismantling the revolution, by force. Recall Orwell's observations quoted above, pages 76–77.

What about Jackson's statement that "the peasants were known to hate the Consejo"? As in the other cases I have cited, Jackson gives no indication of any evidence on which such a judgment might be based. The most detailed investigation of the collectives is from anarchist sources, and they indicate that Aragon was one of the areas where collectivization was most widespread and successful.[57] Both the CNT and the UGT Land Workers' Federation were vigorous in their support for collectivization, and there is no doubt that both were mass organizations. A number of nonanarchists, observing collectivization in Aragon firsthand, gave very favorable reports and stressed the voluntary character of collectivization.[58] According to Gaston Leval, an anarchist observer who carried out detailed investigation of rural collectivization, "in Aragon 75 percent of small proprietors have voluntarily adhered to the new order of things," and others were not forced to involve themselves in collectives.[59] Other anarchist observers— Augustin Souchy in particular—gave detailed observations of the functioning of the Aragon collectives. Unless one is willing to assume a fantastic degree of falsification, it is impossible to reconcile their descriptions with the claim that "the peasants were known to hate the Consejo"—unless, of course,

one restricts the term "peasant" to "individual farm owner,"
in which case it might very well be true, but would justify dis-
banding the Council only on the assumption that the rights of
the individual farm owner must predominate, not those of the
landless worker. There is little doubt that the collectives were
economically successful,[60] hardly likely if collectivization were
forced and hated by the peasantry.

I have already cited Bolloten's general conclusion, based on
very extensive documentary evidence, that while the individual farmer may have viewed the development of collectivized
agriculture with dismay, "the farm workers of the Anarchosyndicalist CNT and the Socialist UGT saw in it, on the contrary,
the commencement of a new era." This conclusion seems
quite reasonable, on the basis of the materials that are available. With respect to Aragon, specifically, he remarks that the
"debt-ridden peasants were strongly affected by the ideas of
the CNT and FAI, a factor that gave a powerful spontaneous
impulse to collective farming," though difficulties are cited by
anarchist sources, which in general appear to be quite honest
about failures. Bolloten cites two Communist sources, among
others, to the effect that about 70 percent of the population in
rural areas of Aragon lived in collectives (p. 71); he adds that
"many of the region's 450 collectives were largely voluntary,"
although "the presence of militiamen from the neighbour-
ing region of Catalonia, the immense majority of whom
were members of the CNT and FAI" was "in some measure"
responsible for the extensive collectivization. He also points
out that in many instances peasant proprietors who were not
compelled to adhere to the collective system did so for other
reasons: ". . . not only were they prevented from employing
hired labour and disposing freely of their crops . . . but they

were often denied all benefits enjoyed by members" (p. 72).
Bolloten cites the attempt of the Communists in April 1937
to cause dissension in "areas where the CNT and UGT had
established collective farms by mutual agreement" (p. 195),
leading in some cases to pitched battles and dozens of assas-
sinations, according to CNT sources.[61]

Bolloten's detailed analysis of the events of the summer of
1937 sheds considerable light on the question of peasant attitudes towards collectivization in Aragon:

> It was inevitable that the attacks on the collectives should
> have had an unfavorable effect upon rural economy and upon
> morale, for while it is true that in some areas collectivization
> was anathema to the majority of peasants, it is no less true
> that in others collective farms were organized spontaneously
> by the bulk of the peasant population. In Toledo province, for
> example, where even before the war rural collectives existed,
> 83 per cent of the peasants, according to a source friendly to
> the Communists, decided in favour of the collective cultiva-
> tion of the soil. As the campaign against the collective farms
> reached its height just before the summer harvest [1937] . . .
> a pall of dismay and apprehension descended upon the agri-
> cultural labourers. Work in the fields was abandoned in many
> places or only carried on apathetically, and there was danger
> that a substantial portion of the harvest, vital for the war effort,
> would be left to rot. [p. 196]

It was under these circumstances, he points out, that the
Communists were forced to change their policy and—
temporarily—to tolerate the collectives. A decree was passed
legalizing collectives *"during the current agricultural year"*

(his italics) and offering them some aid. This "produced a sense of relief in the countryside during the vital period of the harvest." Immediately after the crops had been gathered, the policy changed again to one of harsh repression. Bolloten cites Communist sources to the effect that "a short though fierce campaign at the beginning of August" prepared the way for the dissolution of the Council of Aragon. Following the dissolution decree, "the newly appointed Governor General, José Ignacio Mantecón, a member of the Left Republican Party, but a secret Communist sympathizer [who joined the party in exile, after the war], . . . ordered the break-up of the collective farms." The means: Lister's division, which restored the old order by force and terror. Bolloten cites Communist sources conceding the excessive harshness of Lister's methods. He quotes the Communist general secretary of the Institute of Agrarian Reform, who admits that the measures taken to dissolve the collectives were "a very grave mistake, and produced tremendous disorganization in the countryside," as "those persons who were discontented with the collectives . . . took them by assault, carrying away and dividing up the harvest and farm implements without respecting the collectives that had been formed without violence or pressure, that were prosperous, and that were a model of organization. . . . As a result, labour in the fields was suspended almost entirely, and a quarter of the land had not been prepared at the time for sowing" (p. 200). Once again, it was necessary to ameliorate the harsh repression of the collectives, to prevent disaster. Summarizing these events, Bolloten describes the resulting situation as follows:

> But although the situation in Aragon improved in some degree, the hatreds and resentments generated by the break-up

of the collectives and by the repression that followed were
never wholly dispelled. Nor was the resultant disillusionment that sapped the spirit of the Anarchosyndicalist forces
on the Aragon front ever entirely removed, a disillusionment
that no doubt contributed to the collapse of that front a few
months later . . . after the destruction of the collective farms
in Aragon, the Communist Party was compelled to modify
its policy, and support collectives also in other regions against
former owners who sought the return of confiscated land. . . .
[pp. 200–201]

Returning to Jackson's remarks, I think we must conclude that
they seriously misrepresent the situation.[62] The dissolution
of the Council of Aragon and the large-scale destruction of
the collectives by military force was simply another stage in
the eradication of the popular revolution and the restoration
of the old order. Let me emphasize that I am not criticizing
Jackson for his negative attitude towards the social revolution,
but rather for the failure of objectivity when he deals with the
revolution and the ensuing repression.

Among historians of the Spanish Civil War, the dominant
view is that the Communist policy was in essentials the correct
one—that in order to consolidate domestic and international
support for the Republic it was necessary to block and then
reverse the social revolution. Jackson, for example, states that
Caballero "realized that it was absolutely necessary to rebuild
the authority of the Republican state and to work in close
cooperation with the middle-class liberals." The anarchist
leaders who entered the government shared this view, putting
their trust in the good faith of liberals such as Companys and

believing—naively, as events were to show—that the Western democracies would come to their aid.

A policy diametrically opposed to this was advocated by Camillo Berneri. In his open letter to the anarchist minister Federica Montseny[63] he summarizes his views in the following way: "The dilemma, war or revolution, no longer has meaning. *The only dilemma is this: either victory over Franco through revolutionary war, or defeat*" (his italics). He argued that Morocco should be granted independence and that an attempt should be made to stir up rebellion throughout North Africa. Thus a revolutionary struggle should be undertaken against Western capitalism in North Africa and, simultaneously, against the bourgeois regime in Spain, which was gradually dismantling the accomplishments of the July revolution. The primary front should be political. Franco relied heavily on Moorish contingents, including a substantial number from French Morocco. The Republic might exploit this fact, demoralizing the Nationalist forces and perhaps even winning them to the revolutionary cause by political agitation based on the concrete alternative of pan-Islamic—specifically, Moroccan—revolution. Writing in April 1937, Berneri urged that the army of the Republic be reorganized for the defense of the revolution, so that it might recover the spirit of popular participation of the early days of the revolution. He quotes the words of his compatriot Louis Bertoni, writing from the Huesca front:

> The Spanish war, deprived of all new faith, of any idea of a social transformation, of all revolutionary grandeur, of any universal meaning, is now merely a national war of independence that must be carried on to avoid the extermination that the

international plutocracy demands. There remains a terrible question of life or death, but no longer a war to build a new society and a new humanity.

In such a war, the human element that might bring victory over fascism is lost.

In retrospect, Berneri's ideas seem quite reasonable. Delegations of Moroccan nationalists did in fact approach the Valencia government asking for arms and matériel, but were refused by Caballero, who actually proposed territorial concessions in North Africa to France and England to try to win their support. Commenting on these facts, Broué and Témime observe that these policies deprived the Republic of "the instrument of revolutionary defeatism in the enemy army," and even of a possible weapon against Italian intervention. Jackson, on the other hand, dismisses Berneri's suggestion with the remark that independence for Morocco (as for that matter, even aid to the Moroccan nationalists) was "a gesture that would have been highly appreciated in Paris and London." Of course it is correct that France and Britain would hardly have appreciated this development. As Berneri points out, "it goes without saying that one cannot simultaneously guarantee French and British interests in Morocco and carry out an insurrection." But Jackson's comment does not touch on the central issue, namely, whether the Spanish revolution could have been preserved, both from the fascists at the front and from the bourgeois-Communist coalition within the Republic, by a revolutionary war of the sort that the left proposed—or, for that matter, whether the Republic might not have been saved by a political struggle that involved Franco's invading Moorish troops, or at least eroded their morale. It is easy to see why

Caballero was not attracted by this bold scheme, given his reliance on the eventual backing of the Western democracies. On the basis of what we know today, however, Jackson's summary dismissal of revolutionary war is much too abrupt.

Furthermore, Bertoni's observations from the Huesca front are borne out by much other evidence, some of it cited earlier. Even those who accepted the Communist strategy of discipline and central control as necessary concede that the repressions that formed an ineliminable part of this strategy "tended to break the fighting spirit of the people."[64] One can only speculate, but it seems to me that many commentators have seriously underestimated the significance of the political factor, the potential strength of a popular struggle to defend the achievements of the revolution. It is perhaps relevant that Asturias, the one area of Spain where the system of CNT-UGT committees was not eliminated in favor of central control, is also the one area where guerrilla warfare continued well after Franco's victory. Broué and Témime observe[65] that the resistance of the partisans of Asturias "demonstrates the depth of the revolutionary élan, which had not been shattered by the reinstitution of state authority, conducted here with greater prudence." There can be no doubt that the revolution was both widespread and deeply rooted in the Spanish masses. It seems quite possible that a revolutionary war of the sort advocated by Berneri would have been successful, despite the greater military force of the fascist armies. The idea that men can overcome machines no longer seems as romantic or naive as it may have a few years ago.

Furthermore, the trust placed in the bourgeois government by the anarchist leaders was not honored, as the history of the counterrevolution clearly shows. In retrospect, it seems that Berneri was correct in arguing that they should not have taken part in the bourgeois government, but should rather have sought to replace this government with the institutions created by the revolution.[66] The anarchist minister Garcia Oliver stated that "we had confidence in the word and in the person of a Catalan democrat and retained and supported Companys as President of the Generalitat,"[67] at a time when in Catalonia, at least, the workers' organizations could easily have replaced the state apparatus and dispensed with the former political parties, as they had replaced the old economy with an entirely new structure. Companys recognized fully that there were limits beyond which he could not cooperate with the anarchists. In an interview with H. E. Kaminski, he refused to specify these limits, but merely expressed his hope that "the anarchist masses will not oppose the good sense of their leaders," who have "accepted the responsibilities incumbent upon them"; he saw his task as "directing these responsibilities in the proper path," not further specified in the interview, but shown by the events leading up to the May Days.[68] Probably, Companys' attitude towards this willingness of the anarchist leaders to cooperate was expressed accurately in his reaction to the suggestion of a correspondent of the *New Statesman and Nation*, who predicted that the assassination of the anarchist mayor of Puigcerdá would lead to a revolt: "[Companys] laughed scornfully and said the anarchists would capitulate as they always had before."[69] As has already been pointed out in some detail, the liberal-Communist Party coalition had no intention of letting the war against Franco take precedence over the crushing of the revolution. A spokesman for Comorera put the matter clearly: "This slogan has been attributed to the P.S.U.C.: 'Before taking Saragossa, it is necessary to take

Barcelona.' This reflects the situation exactly. . . ."[70] Comorera himself had, from the beginning, pressed Companys to resist the CNT.[71] The first task of the antifascist coalition, he maintained, was to dissolve the revolutionary committees.[72] I have already cited a good deal of evidence indicating that the repression conducted by the Popular Front seriously weakened popular commitment and involvement in the antifascist war. What was evident to George Orwell was also clear to the Barcelona workers and the peasants in the collectivized villages of Aragon: the liberal-Communist coalition would not tolerate a revolutionary transformation of Spanish society; it would commit itself fully to the anti-Franco struggle only after the old order was firmly re-established, by force, if necessary.[73]

There is little doubt that farm workers in the collectives understood quite well the social content of the drive towards consolidation and central control. We learn this not only from anarchist sources but also from the socialist press in the spring of 1937. On May 1, the Socialist party newspaper *Adelante* had the following to say:

> At the outbreak of the Fascist revolt the labor organizations and the democratic elements in the country were in agreement that the so-called Nationalist Revolution, which threatened to plunge our people into an abyss of deepest misery, could be halted only by a Social Revolution. The Communist Party, however, opposed this view with all its might. It had apparently completely forgotten its old theories of a "workers' and peasants' republic" and a "dictatorship of the proletariat." From its constant repetition of its new slogan of the parliamentary democratic republic it is clear that it has lost all sense of reality. When the Catholic and conservative sections of the

Spanish bourgeoisie saw their old system smashed and could find no way out, the Communist Party instilled new hope into them. It assured them that the democratic bourgeois republic for which it was pleading put no obstacles in the way of Catholic propaganda and, above all, that it stood ready to defend the class interests of the bourgeoisie.[74]

That this realization was widespread in the rural areas was underscored dramatically by a questionnaire sent by *Adelante* to secretaries of the UGT Federation of Land Workers, published in June 1937.[75] The results are summarized as follows:

The replies to these questions revealed an astounding unanimity. Everywhere the same story. The peasant collectives are today most vigorously opposed by the Communist Party. The Communists organize the well-to-do farmers who are on the lookout for cheap labor and are, for this reason, outspokenly hostile to the cooperative undertakings of the poor peasants.

It is the element which before the revolution sympathized with the Fascists and Monarchists which, according to the testimony of the trade-union representatives, is now flocking into the ranks of the Communist Party. As to the general effect of Communist activity on the country, the secretaries of the U.G.T. had only one opinion, which the representative of the Valencia organization put in these words: "It is a misfortune in the fullest sense of the word."[76]

It is not difficult to imagine how the recognition of this "misfortune" must have affected the willingness of the land workers to take part in the antifascist war, with all the sacrifices that this entailed.

The attitude of the central government to the revolution was brutally revealed by its acts and is attested as well in its propaganda. A former minister describes the situation as follows:

> The fact that is concealed by the coalition of the Spanish Communist Party with the left Republicans and right wing Socialists is that there has been a successful social revolution in half of Spain. Successful, that is, in the collectivization of factories and farms which are operated under trade union control, and operated quite efficiently. During the three months that I was director of propaganda for the United States and England under Alvarez del Vayo, then Foreign Minister for the Valencia Government, I was instructed not to send out one word about this revolution in the economic system of loyalist Spain. Nor are any foreign correspondents in Valencia permitted to write freely of the revolution that has taken place.[77]

In short, there is much reason to believe that the will to fight Franco was significantly diminished, perhaps destroyed, by the policy of authoritarian centralization undertaken by the liberal-Communist coalition, carried through by force, and disguised in the propaganda that was disseminated among Western intellectuals[78] and that still dominates the writing of history. To the extent that this is a correct judgment, the alternative proposed by Berneri and the left "extremists" gains in plausibility.

As noted earlier, Caballero and the anarchist ministers accepted the policy of counterrevolution because of their trust in the Western democracies, which they felt sure would sooner or later come to their aid. This feeling was perhaps understandable in 1937. It is strange, however, that a historian writing in the 1960s should dismiss the proposal to strike at Franco's rear by extending the revolutionary war to Morocco, on grounds that this would have displeased Western capitalism (see page 85 above).

Berneri was quite right in his belief that the Western democracies would not take part in an antifascist struggle in Spain. In fact, their complicity in the fascist insurrection was not slight. French bankers, who were generally pro-Franco, blocked the release of Spanish gold to the loyalist government, thus hindering the purchase of arms and, incidentally, increasing the reliance of the Republic on the Soviet Union.[79] The policy of "nonintervention," which effectively blocked Western aid for the loyalist government while Hitler and Mussolini in effect won the war for Franco, was also technically initiated by the French government—though apparently under heavy British pressure.[80]

As far as Great Britain is concerned, the hope that it would come to the aid of the Republic was always unrealistic. A few days after the Franco coup, the foreign editor of *Paris-Soir* wrote: "At least four countries are already taking active interest in the battle—France, which is supporting the Madrid Government, and Britain, Germany and Italy, each of which is giving discreet but nevertheless effective assistance to one group or another among the insurgents."[81] In fact, British support for Franco took a fairly concrete form at the very earliest stages of the insurrection. The Spanish navy remained loyal to the Republic,* and made some attempt to prevent Franco from ferrying troops from Morocco to Spain. Italian

---

* To be more precise, pro-Franco officers were killed, and the seamen remained loyal to the Republic, in many instances.

and German involvement in overcoming these efforts is well documented;[82] the British role has received less attention, but can be determined from contemporary reports. On August 11, 1936, the *New York Times* carried a front-page report on British naval actions in the Straits of Gibraltar, commenting that "this action helps the Rebels by preventing attacks on Algeciras, where troops from Morocco land." (A few days earlier, loyalist warships had bombarded Algeciras, damaging the British consulate.) An accompanying dispatch from Gibraltar describes the situation as it appeared from there:

Angered by the Spanish factions' endangering of shipping and neutral Gibraltar territory in their fighting, Great Britain virtually blockaded Gibraltar Harbor last night with the huge battleship Queen Elizabeth in the center of the entrance, constantly playing searchlights on near-by waters.

Many British warships patrolled the entire Strait today, determined to prevent interference with Britain's control over the entrance to the Mediterranean, a vital place in the British "lifeline to the East."

This action followed repeated warnings to the Spanish Government and yesterday's decree that no more fighting would be permitted in Gibraltar Harbor. The British at Gibraltar had become increasingly nervous after the shelling of Algeciras by the Loyalist battleship Jaime I.

Although British neutrality is still maintained, the patrol of the Strait and the closing of the harbor will aid the military Rebels because Loyalist warships cannot attempt to take Algeciras, now in Rebel hands, and completely isolate the Rebels from Morocco. The Rebels now can release some troops, who were rushed back to Algeciras, for duty further north in the drive for Madrid.

It was reported in Gibraltar tonight that the Rebels had sent a transport across the Strait and had landed more troops from Morocco for use in the columns that are marching northward from headquarters at Seville.

This was the second time this year that Britain warned a power when she believed her measure of Mediterranean control was threatened, and it remains to be seen whether the Madrid Government will flout the British as the Italians did. If it attempts to do so, the British gunners of the Gibraltar fort have authority to fire warning shots. What will happen if such shots go unheeded is obvious.

All the British here refer to the Madrid Government as the "Communists" and there is no doubt where British sympathies now lie, encouraged by the statement of General Francisco Franco, leader of the Rebels, that he is not especially cooperating with Italy.

The British Government has ordered Spaniards here to cease plotting or be expelled and has asked Britons "loyally to refrain from either acting or speaking publicly in such a manner as to display marked partiality or partisanship."

The warning, issued in the official Gibraltar Gazette, was signed by the British Colonial Secretary here.

The warning was issued after reports of possible Communist troubles here had reached official ears and after strong complaints that Spanish Rebels were in Gibraltar. It was said Rebels were making headquarters here and entering La Linea to fight. [Italics mine]

I have quoted this dispatch in full because it conveys rather accurately the character of British "neutrality'" in the early stages of the war and thenceforth. In May 1938, the British ambassador to Spain, Sir Henry Chilton, "expressed the conviction that a Franco victory was necessary for peace in Spain; that there was not the slightest chance that Italy and/or Germany would dominate Spain; and that even if it were possible for the Spanish Government to win (which he did not believe) he was convinced that a victory for Franco would be better for Great Britain."[83] Churchill, who was at first violently opposed to the Republic, modified his position somewhat after the crushing of the revolution in the summer of 1937. What particularly pleased him was the forceful repression of the anarchists and the militarization of the Republic (necessary when "the entire structure of civilization and social life is destroyed," as it had been by the revolution, now happily subdued).[84] However, his good feelings towards the Republic remained qualified. In an interview of August 14, 1938, he expressed himself as follows: "Franco has all the right on his side because he loves his country. Also Franco is defending Europe against the Communist danger—if you wish to put it in those terms. But I, I am English, and I prefer the triumph of the wrong cause. I prefer that the other side wins, because Franco could be an upset or a threat to British interests, and the others no."[85]

The Germans were quite aware of British sentiments, naturally, and therefore were much concerned that the supervisory committee for the nonintervention agreement be located in London rather than Paris. The German Foreign Ministry official responsible for this matter expressed his view on August 29, 1936, as follows: "Naturally, we have to count on complaints of all kinds being brought up in London regarding failure to observe the obligation not to intervene, but we cannot avoid such complaints in any case. It can, in fact, only be agreeable to us if the center of gravity, which after all has thus far been in Paris because of the French initiative, is transferred to London."[86] They were not disappointed. In November, Foreign Secretary Anthony Eden stated in the House of Commons: "So far as breaches [of the nonintervention agreement] are concerned, I wish to state categorically that I think there are other Governments more to blame than those of Germany and Italy."[87] There was no factual basis for this statement, but it did reflect British attitudes. It is interesting that according to German sources, England was at that time supplying Franco with munitions through Gibraltar and, at the same time, providing information to Germany about Russian arms deliveries to the Republic.[88]

The British left was for the most part in support of the liberal-Communist coalition, regarding Caballero as an "infantile leftist" and the anarchists as generally unspeakable.

The British policy of mild support for Franco was to be successful in preserving British interests in Spain, as the Germans soon discovered. A German Foreign Ministry note of October 1937 to the embassy in Nationalist Spain included the following observation: "That England cannot permanently be kept from the Spanish market as in the past is a fact with which we have to reckon. England's old relations with the Spanish mines and the Generalissimo's desire, based on political and economic considerations, to come to an understanding with England place certain limits on our chances of reserving Spanish raw materials to ourselves permanently."[89]

One can only speculate as to what might have been the effects of British support for the Republic. A discussion of this matter would take us far afield, into a consideration of British diplomacy during the late 1930s. It is perhaps worth mention, now that the "Munich analogy" is being bandied about in utter disregard for the historical facts by Secretary Rusk and a number of his academic supporters, that "containment of Communism" was not a policy invented by George Kennan in 1947. Specifically, it was a dominant theme in the diplomacy of the 1930s. In 1934, Lloyd George stated that "in a very short time, perhaps in a year, perhaps in two, the conservative elements in this country will be looking to Germany as the bulwark against Communism in Europe. . . . Do not let us be in a hurry to condemn Germany. We shall be welcoming Germany as our friend."[90] In September 1938, the Munich agreement was concluded; shortly after, both France and Britain did welcome Germany as "our friend." As noted earlier (see note 53), even Churchill's role at this time is subject to some question. Of course, the Munich agreement was the death knell for the Spanish Republic, exactly as the necessity to rely on the Soviet Union signaled the end of the Spanish revolution in 1937.

The United States, like France, exhibited less initiative in these events than Great Britain, which had far more substantial economic interests in Spain and was more of an independent force in European affairs. Nevertheless, the American record is hardly one to inspire pride. Technically, the United States adhered to a position of strict neutrality. However, a careful look raises some doubts. According to information obtained by Jackson, "the American colonel who headed the Telephone Company had placed private lines at the disposal of the Madrid plotters for their conversations with Generals Mola and Franco,"[91] just prior to the insurrection on July 17. In August, the American government urged the Martin Aircraft Company not to honor an agreement made prior to the insurrection to supply aircraft to the Republic, and it also pressured the Mexican government not to reship to Spain war materials purchased in the United States.[92] An American arms exporter, Robert Cuse, insisted on his legal right to ship airplanes and aircraft engines to the Republic in December 1936, and the State Department was forced to grant authorization. Cuse was denounced by Roosevelt as unpatriotic, though Roosevelt was forced to admit that the request was quite legal. Roosevelt contrasted the attitude of other businessmen to Cuse as follows:

> Well, these companies went along with the request of the Government. There is the 90 percent of business that is honest, I mean ethically honest. There is the 90 percent we are always pointing at with pride. And then one man does what amounts to a perfectly legal but thoroughly unpatriotic act. He represents the 10 percent of business that does not live up to the best standards. Excuse the homily, but I feel quite deeply about it.[93]

Among the businesses that remained "ethically honest" and therefore did not incur Roosevelt's wrath was the Texaco Oil Company, which violated its contracts with the Spanish Republic and shipped oil instead to Franco. (Five tankers that were on the high seas in July 1936 were diverted to Franco, who received six million dollars worth of oil on credit during the Civil War.) Apparently, neither the press nor the American government was able to discover this fact, though it was reported in left-wing journals at the time.[94] There is evidence that the American government shared the fears of Churchill and others about the dangerous forces on the Republican side. Secretary of State Cordell Hull, for example, informed Roosevelt on July 23, 1936, that "one of the most serious factors in this situation lies in the fact that the [Spanish] Government has distributed large quantities of arms and ammunition into the hands of irresponsible members of left-wing political organizations."[95]

Like Churchill, many responsible Americans began to rethink their attitude towards the Republic after the social revolution had been crushed.[96] However, relations with Franco continued cordial. In 1957, President Eisenhower congratulated Franco on the "happy anniversary" of his rebellion,[97] and Secretary Rusk added his tribute in 1961. Upon criticism, Rusk was defended by the American ambassador to Madrid, who observed that Spain is "a nation which understands the implacable nature of the communist threat,"[98] like Thailand, South Korea, Taiwan, and selected other countries of the Free World.[99]

In the light of such facts as these, it seems to me that Jackson is not treating the historical record seriously when he dismisses the proposals of the Spanish left as absurd. Quite possibly Berneri's strategy would have failed, as did that of the liberal-Communist coalition that took over the Republic. It was far from senseless, however. I think that the failure of historians to consider it more seriously follows, once again, from the elitist bias that dominates the writing of history—and, in this case, from a certain sentimentality about the Western democracies.

The study of collectivization published by the CNT in 1937[100] concludes with a description of the village of Membrilla. "In its miserable huts live the poor inhabitants of a poor province; eight thousand people, but the streets are not paved, the town has no newspaper, no cinema, neither a café nor a library. On the other hand, it has many churches that have been burned." Immediately after the Franco insurrection, the land was expropriated and village life collectivized. "Food, clothing, and tools were distributed equitably to the whole population. Money was abolished, work collectivized, all goods passed to the community, consumption was socialized. It was, however, not a socialization of wealth but of poverty." Work continued as before. An elected council appointed committees to organize the life of the commune and its relations to the outside world. The necessities of life were distributed freely, insofar as they were available. A large number of refugees were accommodated. A small library was established, and a small school of design.

The document closes with these words:

> The whole population lived as in a large family; functionaries, delegates, the secretary of the syndicates, the members of the municipal council, all elected, acted as heads of a family. But they were controlled, because special privilege or corruption would not be tolerated. Membrilla is perhaps the poorest village of Spain, but it is the most just.

An account such as this, with its concern for human relations and the ideal of a just society, must appear very strange to the consciousness of the sophisticated intellectual, and it is therefore treated with scorn, or taken to be naive or primitive or otherwise irrational. Only when such prejudice is abandoned will it be possible for historians to undertake a serious study of the popular movement that transformed Republican Spain in one of the most remarkable social revolutions that history records.

Franz Borkenau, in commenting on the demoralization caused by the authoritarian practices of the central government, observes (p. 295) that "newspapers are written by Europeanized editors, and the popular movement is inarticulate as to its deepest impulses . . . [which are shown only] . . . by acts." The objectivity of scholarship will remain a delusion as long as these inarticulate impulses remain beyond its grasp. As far as the Spanish revolution is concerned, its history is yet to be written.

I have concentrated on one theme—the interpretation of the social revolution in Spain—in one work of history, a work that is an excellent example of liberal scholarship. It seems to me that there is more than enough evidence to show that a deep bias against social revolution and a commitment to the values and social order of liberal bourgeois democracy has led the author to misrepresent crucial events and to overlook major historical currents. My intention has not been to bring into question the commitment to these values—that is another matter entirely. Rather, it has been to show how this commitment has led to a striking failure of objectivity, providing an example of "counterrevolutionary subordination" of a much more subtle and interesting sort—and ultimately, I believe, a far more important one—than those discussed in the first part of this essay.

4

Interview with Harry Kreisler, from *Political Awakenings*

March 22, 2002

How do you think your parents shaped your perspectives on the world?

Those are always very hard questions, because it's a combination of influence and resistance, which is difficult to sort out. My parents were immigrants, and they happened to end up in Philadelphia, as part of what amounted to kind of a Hebrew ghetto, Jewish ghetto, in Philadelphia. Not a physical ghetto— it was scattered around the city—but a cultural ghetto.

When my father's family came over, for whatever reason, they went to Baltimore, and my mother's family, from another part of the Pale of Settlement, came to New York. The families were totally different. The Baltimore family was ultra-orthodox. In fact, my father told me that they had become more orthodox when they got here than they even were in the shtetl in the Ukraine where they came from. In general, there was a tendency among some sectors of immigrants to intensify the cultural tradition, probably as a way of identifying themselves in a strange environment, I suppose.

The other part of the family, my mother's, was mainly Jewish working class—very radical. The Jewish element had disappeared. This was the 1930s, so they were part of the ferment of radical activism that was going on in all sorts of ways. Of all of them, the one that actually did influence me a great deal was an uncle by marriage who came into the family when I was about seven or eight. He had grown up in a poor area of New York. In fact, he himself never went past fourth grade—on the streets, and with a criminal background, and all [the things that were] going on in the underclass ghettos in New York. He happened to have a physical deformity, so he was able to get a newsstand under a compensation program that was run in the 1930s for people with disabilities. He had a newsstand on 72nd Street in New York and lived nearby in a little apartment. I spent a lot of time there.

That newsstand became an intellectual center for émigrés from Europe; lots of Germans and other émigrés were coming. He wasn't a very educated person, formally—like I said, he never went past fourth grade—but maybe the most educated person I've ever met. Self-educated. The newsstand itself was a very lively, intellectual center—professors of this and that arguing all night. And working at the newsstand was a lot of fun. I went for years thinking that there's a newspaper called *Newsinmira*. Because people came out of the subway station and raced past the newsstand; they would say "Newsinmira," and I gave them two tabloids, which I later discovered were the *News* and the *Mirror*. And I noticed that as soon as they picked up the "Newsinmira," the first thing they opened to was the sports page. So this is an eight-year-old's picture of the world.

There were newspapers there, but that wasn't all there was—that was the background of the discussions that were going on.

Through my uncle and other influences, I got myself involved in the ongoing '30s radicalism, and was very much part of the Hebrew-based, Zionist-oriented—this is Palestine, pre-Israel—Palestine-oriented life. And that was a good part of my life. I became a Hebrew teacher like my parents, and a Zionist youth leader, combining it with the radical activism in various ways. Actually, that's the way I got into linguistics.

You actually wrote your first essay as a ten-year-old, on the Spanish Civil War.

Well, you know, like you said, I was ten years old. I'm sure I would not want to read it today. I remember what it was about because I remember what struck me. This was right after the fall of Barcelona; the fascist forces had conquered Barcelona, and that was essentially the end of the Spanish Civil War. And the article was about the spread of fascism around Europe. So it started off by talking about Munich and Barcelona, and the spread of the Nazi power, fascist power, which was extremely frightening.

Just to add a little word of personal background, we happened to be, for most of my childhood, the only Jewish family in a mostly Irish and German Catholic neighborhood, sort of a lower middle-class neighborhood, which was very anti-Semitic, and quite pro-Nazi. It's obvious why the Irish would be: they hated the British; it's not surprising the Germans were [anti-Semitic]. I can remember beer parties when Paris fell. And the sense of the threat of this black cloud spreading over Europe was very frightening. I could pick up my mother's attitudes, particularly; she was terrified by it.

It was also in my personal life, because I saw the streets. Interesting—for some reason which I do not understand to this day, my brother and I never talked to our parents about it. I don't think they knew that we were living in an anti-Semitic neighborhood. But on the streets, you know, you go out and play ball with kids, or try to walk to the bus or something; it was a constant threat. It was just the kind of thing you knew for some reason not to talk to your parents about. To the day of their death they didn't know. But there was this combination of knowing that this cloud was spreading over the world and picking up, particularly, that my mother was very upset about it—my father too, but more constrained—and living it in the streets in my own daily life, that made it very real.

Anyhow, by the late '30s, I did become quite interested in Spanish anarchism and the Spanish Civil War, where all of this was being fought out at the time. Right before the World War broke out, a kind of microcosm was going on in Spain. By the time I was old enough to get on a train by myself, around ten or eleven, I would go to New York for a weekend and stay with my aunt and uncle, and hang around at anarchist bookstores down around Union Square and Fourth Avenue. There were little bookstores with émigrés, really interesting people. To my mind they looked about ninety; they were maybe in their forties or something, and they were very interested in young people. They wanted young people to come along, so they spent a lot of attention. Talking to these people was a real education.

These experiences we've described, you were saying they led you into linguistics, but also led you into your view of politics and of the world. You're a libertarian anarchist, and when one hears

that, because of the way issues are framed in this country, there
are many misperceptions. Help us understand what that means.

The United States is sort of out of the world on this topic.
Here, the term "libertarian" means the opposite of what it
always meant in history. Libertarian throughout modern
European history meant socialist anarchist. It meant the antistate element of the Workers' Movement and the Socialist
Movement. Here it means ultra-conservative—Ayn Rand or
Cato Institute or something like that. But that's a special U.S.
usage. There are a lot of things quite special about the way the
United States developed, and this is part of it. In Europe, it
meant, and always meant to me, an antistate branch of socialism, which meant a highly organized society, nothing to do
with chaos, but based on democracy all the way through. That
means democratic control of communities, of workplaces, of
federal structures, built on systems of voluntary association,
spreading internationally. That's traditional anarchism. You
know, anybody can have the word if they like, but that's the
mainstream of traditional anarchism.

And it has roots. Coming back to the United States, it has
very strong roots in the American working-class movements.
So if you go back to, say, the 1850s, the beginnings of the Industrial Revolution, right around the area where I live, in Eastern Massachusetts, in the textile plants and so on, the people
working on those plants were, in part, young women coming
off the farm. They were called "factory girls," the women from
the farms who worked in the textile plants. Some of them
were Irish, immigrants in Boston and that group of people.
They had an extremely rich and interesting culture. They're
kind of like my uncle who never went past fourth grade—very

educated, reading modern literature. They didn't bother with European radicalism; that had no effect on them, but they were very much a part of the general literary culture. And they developed their own conceptions of how the world ought to be organized.

They had their own newspapers. In fact, the period of the freest press in the United States was probably around the 1850s. In the 1850s, the scale of the popular press—meaning run by factory girls in Lowell and so on—was on the scale of the commercial press or even greater. These were independent newspapers that [arose] spontaneously, without any background. [The writers had] never heard of Marx or Bakunin or anyone else, yet they developed the same ideas. From their point of view, what they called "wage slavery," renting yourself to an owner, was not very different from the chattel slavery that they were fighting a civil war about. So the idea of renting yourself, meaning working for wages, was degrading. It was an attack on your personal integrity. They despised the industrial system that was developing, that was destroying their culture, destroying their independence, their individuality, constraining them to be subordinate to masters.

There was a tradition of what was called Republicanism in the United States. We're free people, you know, the first free people in the world. This was destroying and undermining that freedom. This was the core of the labor movement all over, and included in it was the assumption, just taken for granted, that those who work in the mills should own them.

In fact, one of their main slogans was a condemnation of what they called the "new spirit of the age: gain wealth, forgetting all but self." That new spirit, that you should only be interested in gaining wealth and forgetting about your relations to other people, they regarded it as a violation of fundamental human nature and a degrading idea.

That was a strong, rich American culture, which was crushed by violence. The United States has a very violent labor history, much more so than Europe. It was wiped out over a long period, with extreme violence. By the time it picked up again in the 1930s, that's when I personally came into the tail end of it. After the Second World War it was crushed. By now, it's forgotten. But it's very real. I don't really think it's forgotten; I think it's just below the surface in people's consciousness.

You examine in your work the extent to which histories and traditions are forgotten. To define a new position often means going back and finding those older traditions.

Things like this, they're forgotten in the intellectual culture, but my feeling is they're alive in the popular culture, in people's sentiments and attitudes and understanding and so on. I know when I talk to, say, working-class audiences today, and I talk about these ideas, they seem very natural to them. It's true, nobody talks about them, but when you bring up the idea that you have to rent yourself to somebody and follow their orders, and that they own and you work—you built it, but you don't own it—that's a highly unnatural notion. You don't have to study any complicated theories to see that this is an attack on human dignity.

So coming out of this tradition, being influenced by and continuing to believe in it, what is your notion of legitimate power? Under what circumstances is power legitimate?

The core of the anarchist tradition, as I understand it, is that power is always illegitimate, unless it proves itself to be legitimate. So the burden of proof is always on those who claim that some authoritarian hierarchic relation is legitimate. If they can't prove it, then it should be dismantled.

Can you ever prove it? Well, it's a heavy burden of proof to bear, but I think sometimes you can bear it. So to take an example, if I'm walking down the street with my four-year-old granddaughter, and she starts to run into the street, and I grab her arm and pull her back, that's an exercise of power and authority, but I can give a justification for it, and it's obvious what the justification would be. And maybe there are other cases where you can justify it. But the question that always should be asked uppermost in our mind is, "Why should I accept it?" It's the responsibility of those who exercise power to show that somehow it's legitimate. It's not the responsibility of anyone else to show that it's illegitimate. It's illegitimate by assumption, if it's a relation of authority among human beings which places some above others. Unless you can give a strong argument to show that it's right, you've lost.

It's kind of like the use of violence, say, in international affairs. There's a very heavy burden of proof to be borne by anyone who calls for violence. Maybe it can be sometimes justified. Personally, I'm not a committed pacifist, so I think that, yes, it can sometimes be justified. So I thought, in fact, in that article I wrote in fourth grade, I thought the West should be using force to try to stop Fascism, and I still think so. But now I know a lot more about it. I know that the West was actually supporting Fascism, supporting Franco, supporting Mussolini, and so on, and even Hitler. I didn't know that at the time. But I thought then and I think now that the use of force to stop that plague would have been legitimate, and finally was legitimate. But an argument has to be given for it.

You've said, "You can lie or distort the story of the French Revolution as long as you like and nothing will happen. Propose a false theory in chemistry and it will be refuted tomorrow." How does your approach to the world as a scientist affect and influence the way you approach politics?

Nature is tough. You can't fiddle with Mother Nature, she's a hard taskmistress. So you're forced to be honest in the natural sciences. In the soft fields, you're not forced to be honest. There are standards, of course; on the other hand, they're very weak. If what you propose is ideologically acceptable, that is, supportive of power systems, you can get away with a huge amount. In fact, the difference between the conditions that are imposed on dissident opinion and on mainstream opinion is radically different.

For example, I've written about terrorism, and I think you can show without much difficulty that terrorism pretty much corresponds to power. I don't think that's very surprising. The more powerful states are involved in more terrorism, by and large. The United States is the most powerful, so it's involved in massive terrorism, by its own definition of terrorism. Well, if I want to establish that, I'm required to give a huge amount of evidence. I think that's a good thing. I don't object to that. I think anyone who makes that claim should be held to very high standards. So, I do extensive documentation, from the internal secret records and historical record and so on. And if you ever find a comma misplaced, somebody ought to criticize you for it. So I think those standards are fine.

All right, now, let's suppose that you play the mainstream game. You can say anything you want because you support power, and nobody expects you to justify anything. For example, in the unimaginable circumstance that I was on, say, *Nightline*, and I was asked, "Do you think Kadhafi is a terrorist?" I could say, "Yeah, Kadhafi is a terrorist." I don't need any evidence. Suppose I said, "George Bush is a terrorist." Well, then I would be expected to provide evidence—"Why would you say that?"

In fact, the structure of the news production system is, you can't produce evidence. There's even a name for it—I learned it from the producer of *Nightline*, Jeff Greenfield. It's called "concision." He was asked in an interview somewhere why they didn't have me on *Nightline*. First of all, he says, "Well, he talks Turkish, and nobody understands it." But the other answer was, "He lacks concision." Which is correct, I agree with him. The kinds of things that I would say on *Nightline*, you can't say in one sentence because they depart from standard religion. If you want to repeat the religion, you can get away with it between two commercials. If you want to say something that questions the religion, you're expected to give evidence, and that you can't do between two commercials. So therefore you lack concision, so therefore you can't talk.

I think that's a terrific technique of propaganda. To impose concision is a way of virtually guaranteeing that the party line gets repeated over and over again, and that nothing else is heard.

What is your advice for people who have the same concerns, who identify with the tradition that you come out of, and who want to be engaged in opposition?

The same as the factory girls in the Lowell textile plant 150 years ago: they joined with others. To do these things alone is extremely hard, especially when you're working fifty hours a week to put the food on the table. Join with others, and you can do a lot of things. It's got a big multiplier effect. That's why unions have always been in the lead of development of social and economic progress. They bring together poor people, working people, enable them to learn from one another, to have their own sources of information, and to act collectively. That's how everything is changed—the civil rights movement, the feminist movement, the solidarity movements, the workers' movements. The reason we don't live in a dungeon is because people have joined together to change things. And there's nothing different now from before. In fact, just in the last forty years, we've seen remarkable changes in this respect.

Go back to '62, there was no feminist movement, there was a very limited human rights movement. There was no environmental movement, meaning rights of our grandchildren. There were no Third World solidarity movements. There was no antiapartheid movement. There was no anti-sweatshop movement. I mean, all of the things that we take for granted just weren't there. How did they get there? Was it a gift from an angel? No, they got there by struggle, common struggle by people who dedicated themselves with others, because you can't do it alone, and [their efforts] made it a much more civilized country. It was a long way to go, and that's not the first time it happened. And it will continue.

You believe that when we focus on heroes in the movement, that's a mistake, because it's really the unsung heroes, the unsung

*seamstresses or whatever in this movement, who actually make
a difference.*

Take, say, the civil rights movement. When you think of the
civil rights movement, the first thing you think of is Martin
Luther King Jr. King was an important figure. But he would
have been the first to tell you, I'm sure, that he was riding the
wave of activism, that people who were doing the work, who
were in the lead in the civil rights movement, were young
SNCC [Student Nonviolent Coordinating Committee] workers, freedom riders, people out there in the streets every day
getting beaten and sometimes killed, working constantly. They
created the circumstances in which a Martin Luther King
could come in and be a leader. His role was extremely important, I'm not denigrating it, it was very important to have done
that. But the people who were really important are the ones
whose names are forgotten. And that's true of every movement
that ever existed.

*Is it the case that by seeing so much you understand that very
little sometimes can be accomplished, but that may be very
important?*

I don't think we should give up long-term visions. I agree with
the factory girls in Lowell in 1850. I think wage slavery is an
attack on fundamental human rights. I think those who work
in the plants should own them. I think we should struggle
against what was then the "new spirit of the age": gain wealth,
forgetting everybody but yourself. Yes, that's all degrading
and destructive, and in the long term—I don't know how
long—it should be dismantled. But right now there are serious

problems to deal with, like thirty million Americans who don't have enough to eat, or people elsewhere in the world who are far worse off, and who are, in fact, under our boot, we're grinding them into the dust. Those are short-term things that can be dealt with. There's nothing wrong with making small gains, like the gains that I was talking about before, from the '60s until today. They're extremely important for human lives. It doesn't mean that there are not a lot of mountain peaks to climb, there are. But you do what's within range.

The same in the sciences. You might like to solve the problems of, say, what causes human action, but the problems you work on are the ones that are right at the edge of your understanding. There's a famous joke about a drunk under a lamppost looking at the ground, and somebody comes up and asks him "What are you looking for?" He says, "I'm looking for a pencil that I dropped." They say, "Well, where did you drop it?" He says, "Oh, I dropped it across the street." "Well, why are looking here?" "This is where the light is." That's the way the sciences work. Maybe the problem you would like to solve is across the street, but you have to work where the light is. If you try to move it a little farther, maybe ultimately you'll get across the street.

5

Language and Freedom

When I was invited to speak on the topic "language and freedom," I was puzzled and intrigued. Most of my professional life has been devoted to the study of language. There would be no great difficulty in finding a topic to discuss in that domain. And there is much to say about the problems of freedom and liberation as they pose themselves to us and to others in the mid-twentieth century. What is troublesome in the title of this lecture is the conjunction. In what way are language and freedom to be interconnected?

As a preliminary, let me say just a word about the contemporary study of language, as I see it. There are many aspects of language and language use that raise intriguing questions, but—in my judgment—only a few have so far led to productive theoretical work. In particular, our deepest insights are in the area of formal grammatical structure. A person who knows a language has acquired a system of rules and principles— a "generative grammar," in technical terms—that associates sound and meaning in some specific fashion. There are many reasonably well-founded and, I think, rather enlightening hypotheses as to the character of such grammars, for quite

a number of languages. Furthermore, there has been a re-
newal of interest in "universal grammar," interpreted now as
the theory that tries to specify the general properties of these
languages that can be learned in the normal way by humans.
Here too, significant progress has been achieved. The subject
is of particular importance. It is appropriate to regard universal grammar as the study of one of the essential faculties
of mind. It is, therefore, extremely interesting to discover, as
I believe we do, that the principles of universal grammar are
rich, abstract, and restrictive, and can be used to construct
principled explanations for a variety of phenomena. At the
present stage of our understanding, if language is to provide a
springboard for the investigation of other problems of man, it
is these aspects of language to which we will have to turn our
attention, for the simple reason that it is only these aspects that
are reasonably well understood. In another sense, the study of
formal properties of language reveals something of the nature
of man in a negative way: it underscores, with great clarity,
the limits of our understanding of those qualities of mind that
are apparently unique to man and that must enter into his
cultural achievements in an intimate, if still quite obscure,
manner.

In searching for a point of departure, one turns naturally to
a period in the history of Western thought when it was possible
to believe that "the thought of making freedom the sum and
substance of philosophy has emancipated the human spirit in
all its relationships, and . . . has given to science in all its parts
a more powerful reorientation than any earlier revolution."[1]
The word "revolution" bears multiple associations in this passage, for Schelling also proclaims that "man is born to act and
not to speculate"; and when he writes that "the time has come

to proclaim to a nobler humanity the freedom of the spirit, and no longer to have patience with men's tearful regrets for their lost chains," we hear the echoes of the libertarian thought and revolutionary acts of the late eighteenth century. Schelling writes that "the beginning and end of all philosophy is—Freedom." These words are invested with meaning and urgency at a time when men are struggling to cast off their chains, to resist authority that has lost its claim to legitimacy, to construct more humane and more democratic social institutions. It is at such a time that the philosopher may be driven to inquire into the nature of human freedom and its limits, and perhaps to conclude, with Schelling, that with respect to the human ego, "its essence is freedom"; and with respect to philosophy, "the highest dignity of Philosophy consists precisely therein, that it stakes all on human freedom."

We are living, once again, at such a time. A revolutionary ferment is sweeping the so-called Third World, awakening enormous masses from torpor and acquiescence in traditional authority. There are those who feel that the industrial societies as well are ripe for revolutionary change—and I do not refer only to representatives of the New Left. See for example, the remarks of Paul Ricoeur cited in chapter 6 [of *For Reasons of State*], pages 308–9.

The threat of revolutionary change brings forth repression and reaction. Its signs are evident in varying forms, in France, in the Soviet Union, in the United States—not least, in the city where we are meeting. It is natural, then, that we should consider, abstractly, the problems of human freedom, and turn with interest and serious attention to the thinking of an earlier period when archaic social institutions were subjected to critical analysis and sustained attack. It is natural and appropriate, so long as we bear in mind Schelling's admonition, that man is born not merely to speculate but also to act.

One of the earliest and most remarkable of the eighteenth-century investigations of freedom and servitude is Rousseau's *Discourse on Inequality* (1755), in many ways a revolutionary tract. In it, he seeks to "set forth the origin and progress of inequality, the establishment and abuse of political societies, insofar as these things can be deduced from the nature of man by the light of reason alone." His conclusions were sufficiently shocking that the judges of the prize competition of the Academy of Dijon, to whom the work was originally submitted, refused to hear the manuscript through.[2] In it, Rousseau challenges the legitimacy of virtually every social institution, as well as individual control of property and wealth. These are "usurpations . . . established only on a precarious and abusive right. . . . having been acquired only by force, force could take them away without [the rich] having grounds for complaint." Not even property acquired by personal industry is held "upon better titles." Against such a claim, one might object: "Do you not know that a multitude of your brethren die or suffer from need of what you have in excess, and that you needed express and unanimous consent of the human race to appropriate for yourself anything from common subsistence that exceeded your own?" It is contrary to the law of nature that "a handful of men be glutted with superfluities while the starving multitude lacks necessities."

Rousseau argues that civil society is hardly more than a conspiracy by the rich to guarantee their plunder. Hypocritically, the rich call upon their neighbors to "institute regulations of justice and peace to which all are obliged to conform, which make an exception of no one, and which compensate in some way for the caprices of fortune by equally subjecting the powerful and the weak to mutual duties"—those laws which, as Anatole France was to say, in their majesty deny to the rich and the poor equally the right to sleep under the bridge at night. By such arguments, the poor and weak were seduced: "All ran to meet their chains thinking they secured their freedom. . . ." Thus society and laws "gave new fetters to the weak and new forces to the rich, destroyed natural freedom for all time, established forever the law of property and inequality, changed a clever usurpation into an irrevocable right, and for the profit of a few ambitious men henceforth subjected the whole human race to work, servitude and misery." Governments inevitably tend towards arbitrary power, as "their corruption and extreme limit." This power is "by its nature illegitimate," and new revolutions must

> dissolve the government altogether or bring it closer to its legitimate institution. . . . The uprising that ends by strangling or dethroning a sultan is as lawful an act as those by which he disposed, the day before, of the lives and goods of his subjects. Force alone maintained him, force alone overthrows him.

What is interesting, in the present connection, is the path that Rousseau follows to reach these conclusions "by the light of reason alone," beginning with his ideas about the nature of man. He wants to see man "as nature formed him." It is from the nature of man that the principles of natural right and the foundations of social existence must be deduced.

> This same study of original man, of his true needs, and of the principles underlying his duties, is also the only good means

one could use to remove those crowds of difficulties which present themselves concerning the origin of moral inequality, the true foundation of the body politic, the reciprocal rights of its members, and a thousand similar questions as important as they are ill explained.

To determine the nature of man, Rousseau proceeds to compare man and animal. Man is "intelligent, free . . . the sole animal endowed with reason." Animals are "devoid of intellect and freedom."

In every animal I see only an ingenious machine to which nature has given senses in order to revitalize itself and guarantee itself, to a certain point, from all that tends to destroy or upset it. I perceive precisely the same things in the human machine, with the difference that nature alone does everything in the operations of a beast, whereas man contributes to his operations by being a free agent. The former chooses or rejects by instinct and the latter by an act of freedom, so that a beast cannot deviate from the rule that is prescribed to it even when it would be advantageous for it to do so, and a man deviates from it often to his detriment . . . it is not so much understanding which constitutes the distinction of man among the animals as it is his being a free agent. Nature commands every animal, and the beast obeys. Man feels the same impetus, but he realizes that he is free to acquiesce or resist; and it is above all in the consciousness of this freedom that the spirituality of his soul is shown. For physics explains in some way the mechanism of the senses and the formation of ideas; but in the power of willing, or rather of choosing, and in the sentiment of this power are found only purely spiritual acts about which the laws of mechanics explain nothing.

Thus the essence of human nature is man's freedom and his consciousness of his freedom. So Rousseau can say that "the jurists, who have gravely pronounced that the child of a slave would be born a slave, have decided in other terms that a man would not be born a man."[3]

Sophistic politicians and intellectuals search for ways to obscure the fact that the essential and defining property of man is his freedom: "they attribute to men a natural inclination to servitude, without thinking that it is the same for freedom as for innocence and virtue—their value is felt only as long as one enjoys them oneself and the taste for them is lost as soon as one has lost them." In contrast, Rousseau asks rhetorically "whether, freedom being the most noble of man's faculties, it is not degrading one's nature, putting oneself on the level of beasts enslaved by instinct, even offending the author of one's being, to renounce without reservation the most precious of all his gifts and subject ourselves to committing all the crimes he forbids us in order to please a ferocious or insane master"— a question that has been asked, in similar terms, by many an American draft resister in the last few years, and by many others who are beginning to recover from the catastrophe of twentieth-century Western civilization, which has so tragically confirmed Rousseau's judgment:

> Hence arose the national wars, battles, murders, and reprisals which make nature tremble and shock reason, and all those horrible prejudices which rank the honor of shedding human blood among the virtues. The most decent men learned to

consider it one of their duties to murder their fellowmen; at length men were seen to massacre each other by the thousands without knowing why; more murders were committed on a single day of fighting and more horrors in the capture of a single city than were committed in the state of nature during whole centuries over the entire face of the earth.

The proof of his doctrine that the struggle for freedom is an essential human attribute, that the value of freedom is felt only as long as one enjoys it, Rousseau sees in "the marvels done by all free peoples to guard themselves from oppression." True, those who have abandoned the life of a free man

do nothing but boast incessantly of the peace and repose they enjoy in their chains. . . . But when I see the others sacrifice pleasures, repose, wealth, power, and life itself for the preservation of this sole good which is so disdained by those who have lost it; when I see animals born free and despising captivity break their heads against the bars of their prison; when I see multitudes of entirely naked savages scorn European voluptuousness and endure hunger, fire, the sword, and death to preserve only their independence, I feel that it does not behoove slaves to reason about freedom.

Rather similar thoughts were expressed by Kant, forty years later. He cannot, he says, accept the proposition that certain people "are not ripe for freedom," for example, the serfs of some landlord.

If one accepts this assumption, freedom will never be achieved; for one can not arrive at the maturity for freedom without having already acquired it; one must be free to learn how to make use of one's powers freely and usefully. The first attempts will surely be brutal and will lead to a state of affairs more painful and dangerous than the former condition under the dominance but also the protection of an external authority. However, one can achieve reason only through one's own experiences and one must be free to be able to undertake them. . . . To accept the principle that freedom is worthless for those under one's control and that one has the right to refuse it to them forever, is an infringement on the rights of God himself, who has created man to be free.[4]

The remark is particularly interesting because of its context. Kant was defending the French Revolution, during the Terror, against those who claimed that it showed the masses to be unready for the privilege of freedom. Kant's remarks have contemporary relevance. No rational person will approve of violence and terror. In particular, the terror of the post-revolutionary state, fallen into the hands of a grim autocracy, has more than once reached indescribable levels of savagery. Yet no person of understanding or humanity will too quickly condemn the violence that often occurs when long-subdued masses rise against their oppressors, or take their first steps towards liberty and social reconstruction.

Let me return now to Rousseau's argument against the legitimacy of established authority, whether that of political power or of wealth. It is striking that his argument, up to this point, follows a familiar Cartesian model. Man is uniquely beyond the bounds of physical explanation; the beast, on the other hand, is merely an ingenious machine, commanded by natural law. Man's freedom and his consciousness of this freedom distinguish him from the beast-machine. The principles of mechanical explanation are incapable of accounting for these human properties, though they can account for sensation and even the combination of ideas, in which regard "man differs from a beast only in degree."

To Descartes and his followers, such as Cordemoy, the only sure sign that another organism has a mind, and hence also lies beyond the bounds of mechanical explanation, is its use of language in the normal, creative human fashion, free from control by identifiable stimuli, novel and innovative, appropriate to situations, coherent, and engendering in our minds new thoughts and ideas.[5] To the Cartesians, it is obvious by introspection that each man possesses a mind, a substance whose essence is thought; his creative use of language reflects this freedom of thought and conception. When we have evidence that another organism too uses language in this free and creative fashion, we are led to attribute to it as well a mind like ours. From similar assumptions regarding the intrinsic limits of mechanical explanation, its inability to account for man's freedom and consciousness of his freedom, Rousseau proceeds to develop his critique of authoritarian institutions, which deny to man his essential attribute of freedom, in varying degree.

Were we to combine these speculations, we might develop an interesting connection between language and freedom. Language, in its essential properties and the manner of its use, provides the basic criterion for determining that another organism is a being with a human mind and the human capacity for free thought and self-expression, and with the essential human need for freedom from the external constraints of repressive authority. Furthermore, we might try to proceed from the detailed investigation of language and its use to a deeper and more specific understanding of the human mind. Proceeding on this model, we might further attempt to study other aspects of that human nature which, as Rousseau rightly observes, must be correctly conceived if we are to be able to develop, in theory, the foundations for a rational social order.

I will return to this problem, but first I would like to trace further Rousseau's thinking about the matter. Rousseau diverges from the Cartesian tradition in several respects. He defines the "specific characteristic of the human species" as man's "faculty of self-perfection," which, "with the aid of circumstances, successively develops all the others, and resides among us as much in the species as in the individual." The faculty of self-perfection and of perfection of the human species through cultural transmission is not, to my knowledge, discussed in any similar terms by the Cartesians. However, I think that Rousseau's remarks might be interpreted as a development of the Cartesian tradition in an unexplored direction, rather than as a denial and rejection of it. There is no inconsistency in the notion that the restrictive attributes of mind underlie a historically evolving human nature that develops within the limits that they set; or that these attributes of mind provide the possibility for self-perfection; or that, by providing the consciousness of freedom, these essential attributes of human nature give man the opportunity to create social conditions and social forms to maximize the possibilities for freedom, diversity, and individual self-realization. To use an arithmetical analogy, the integers do not fail to be an infinite set merely because they do not exhaust the rational numbers. Analogously, it is no denial of man's capacity for infinite "self-perfection" to hold that there are intrinsic properties of mind that constrain his development. I would like to argue that in a sense the opposite is true, that without a system of formal constraints there are no creative acts; specifically, in the absence of intrinsic and restrictive properties of mind, there can be only "shaping of behavior" but no creative acts of self-perfection. Furthermore, Rousseau's concern for the evolutionary character of self-perfection brings us back, from another point of view, to a concern for human language, which would appear to be a prerequisite for such evolution of society and culture, for Rousseau's perfection of the species, beyond the most rudimentary forms.

Rousseau holds that "although the organ of speech is natural to man, speech itself is nonetheless not natural to him." Again, I see no inconsistency between this observation and the typical Cartesian view that innate abilities are "dispositional," faculties that lead us to produce ideas (specifically, innate ideas) in a particular manner under given conditions of external stimulation, but that also provide us with the ability to proceed in our thinking without such external factors. Language too, then, is natural to man only in a specific way. This is an important and, I believe, quite fundamental insight of the rationalist linguists that was disregarded, very largely, under the impact of empiricist psychology in the eighteenth century and since.[6]

Rousseau discusses the origin of language at some length, though he confesses himself to be unable to come to grips with the problem in a satisfactory way. Thus

if men needed speech in order to learn to think, they had even greater need of knowing how to think in order to discover the art of speech. . . . So that one can hardly form tenable

conjectures about this art of communicating thoughts and
establishing intercourse between minds; a sublime art which is
now very far from its origin. . . .

He holds that "general ideas can come into the mind only
with the aid of words, and the understanding grasps them only
through propositions"—a fact which prevents animals, devoid
of reason, from formulating such ideas or ever acquiring "the
perfectiblity which depends upon them." Thus he cannot conceive of the means by which "our new grammarians began to
extend their ideas and to generalize their words," or to develop
the means "to express all the thoughts of men": "numbers, abstract words, aorists, and all the tenses of verbs, particles, syntax, the linking of propositions, reasoning, and the forming of
all the logic of discourse." He does speculate about later stages
of the perfection of the species, "when the ideas of men began
to spread and multiply, and when closer communication was
established among them, [and] they sought more numerous
signs and a more extensive language." But he must, unhappily,
abandon "the following difficult problem: which was most
necessary, previously formed society for the institution of languages, or previously invented languages for the establishment
of society?"

The Cartesians cut the Gordian knot by postulating the
existence of a species-specific characteristic, a second substance that serves as what we might call a "creative principle"
alongside the "mechanical principle" that determines totally
the behavior of animals. There was, for them, no need to
explain the origin of language in the course of historical evolution. Rather, man's nature is qualitatively distinct: there is no
passage from body to mind. We might reinterpret this idea in

more current terms by speculating that rather sudden and dramatic mutations might have led to qualities of intelligence that are, so far as we know, unique to man, possession of language in the human sense being the most distinctive index of these qualities.[7] If this is correct, as at least a first approximation to the facts, the study of language might be expected to offer an entering wedge, or perhaps a model, for an investigation of human nature that would provide the grounding for a much broader theory of human nature.

To conclude these historical remarks, I would like to turn, as I have elsewhere,[8] to Wilhelm von Humboldt, one of the most stimulating and intriguing thinkers of the period. Humboldt was, on the one hand, one of the most profound theorists of general linguistics, and on the other, an early and forceful advocate of libertarian values. The basic concept of his philosophy is *Bildung*, by which, as J. W. Burrow expresses it, "he meant the fullest, richest and most harmonious development of the potentialities of the individual, the community or the human race."[9] His own thought might serve as an exemplary case. Though he does not, to my knowledge, explicitly relate his ideas about language to his libertarian social thought, there is quite clearly a common ground from which they develop, a concept of human nature that inspires each. Mill's essay *On Liberty* takes as its epigraph Humboldt's formulation of the "leading principle" of his thought: "the absolute and essential importance of human development in its richest diversity." Humboldt concludes his critique of the authoritarian state by saying: "I have felt myself animated throughout with a sense of the deepest respect for the inherent dignity of human nature, and for freedom, which alone befits that dignity." Briefly put, his concept of human nature is this:

The true end of Man, or that which is prescribed by the eternal and immutable dictates of reason, and not suggested by vague and transient desires, is the highest and most harmonious development of his powers to a complete and consistent whole. Freedom is the first and indispensable condition which the possibility of such a development presupposes; but there is besides another essential—intimately connected with freedom, it is true—a variety of situations.[10]

Like Rousseau and Kant, he holds that

nothing promotes this ripeness for freedom so much as freedom itself. This truth, perhaps, may not be acknowledged by those who have so often used this unripeness as an excuse for continuing repression. But it seems to me to follow unquestionably from the very nature of man. The incapacity for freedom can only arise from a want of moral and intellectual power; to heighten this power is the only way to supply this want; but to do this presupposes the exercise of the power, and this exercise presupposes the freedom which awakens spontaneous activity. Only it is clear we cannot call it giving freedom, when bonds are relaxed which are not felt as such by him who wears them. But of no man on earth—however neglected by nature, and however degraded by circumstances—is this true of all the bonds which oppress him. Let us undo them one by one, as the feeling of freedom awakens in men's hearts, and we shall hasten progress at every step.

Those who do not comprehend this "may justly be suspected of misunderstanding human nature, and of wishing to make men into machines."

Man is fundamentally a creative, searching, self-perfecting being: "to inquire and to create—these are the centres around which all human pursuits more or less directly revolve." But freedom of thought and enlightenment are not only for the elite. Once again echoing Rousseau, Humboldt states: "There is something degrading to human nature in the idea of refusing to any man the right to be a man." He is, then, optimistic about the effects on all of "the diffusion of scientific knowledge by freedom and enlightenment." But "all moral culture springs solely and immediately from the inner life of the soul, and can only be stimulated in human nature, and never produced by external and artificial contrivances." "The cultivation of the understanding, as of any of man's other faculties, is generally achieved by his own activity, his own ingenuity, or his own methods of using the discoveries of others. . . ." Education, then, must provide the opportunities for self-fulfillment; it can at best provide a rich and challenging environment for the individual to explore, in his own way. Even a language cannot, strictly speaking, be taught, but only "awakened in the mind: one can only provide the thread along which it will develop of itself." I think that Humboldt would have found congenial much of Dewey's thinking about education. And he might also have appreciated the recent revolutionary extension of such ideas, for example, by the radical Catholics of Latin America who are concerned with the "awakening of consciousness," referring to "the transformation of the passive exploited lower classes into conscious and critical masters of their own destinies"[11] much in the manner of Third World revolutionaries elsewhere. He would, I am sure, have approved of their criticism of schools that are more preoccupied with the transmission of knowledge than with the creation, among other values, of a critical spirit. From the social point of view, the educational systems are oriented to maintaining the existing social and economic structures instead of transforming them.[12]

But Humboldt's concern for spontaneity goes well beyond educational practice in the narrow sense. It touches also the question of labor and exploitation. The remarks, just quoted, about the cultivation of understanding through spontaneous action continue as follows:

> . . . man never regards what he possesses as so much his own, as what he does; and the labourer who tends a garden is perhaps in a truer sense its owner, than the listless voluptuary who enjoys its fruits. . . . In view of this consideration,[13] it seems as if all peasants and craftsmen might be elevated into artists; that is, men who love their labour for its own sake, improve it by their own plastic genius and inventive skill, and thereby cultivate their intellect, ennoble their character, and exalt and refine their pleasures. And so humanity would be ennobled by the very things which now, though beautiful in themselves, so often serve to degrade it. . . . But, still, freedom is undoubtedly the indispensable condition, without which even the pursuits most congenial to individual human nature, can never succeed in producing such salutary influences. Whatever does not spring from a man's free choice, or is only the result of instruction and guidance, does not enter into his very being, but remains alien to his true nature; he does not perform it with truly human energies, but merely with mechanical exactness.

If a man acts in a purely mechanical way, reacting to external demands or instruction rather than in ways determined by his own interests and energies and power, "we may admire what he does, but we despise what he is." [14]

On such conceptions Humboldt grounds his ideas concerning the role of the state, which tends to "make man an instrument to serve its arbitrary ends, overlooking his individual purposes." His doctrine is classical liberal, strongly opposed to all but the most minimal forms of state intervention in personal or social life.

Writing in the 1790s, Humboldt had no conception of the forms that industrial capitalism would take. Hence he is not overly concerned with the dangers of private power.

> But when we reflect (still keeping theory distinct from practice) that the influence of a private person is liable to diminution and decay, from competition, dissipation of fortune, even death; and that clearly none of these contingencies can be applied to the State; we are still left with the principle that the latter is not to meddle in anything which does not refer exclusively to security. . . .

He speaks of the essential equality of the condition of private citizens, and of course has no idea of the ways in which the notion "private person" would come to be reinterpreted in the era of corporate capitalism. He did not foresee that "Democracy with its motto of *equality of all citizens before the law* and Liberalism with its *right of man over his own person* both [would be] wrecked on realities of capitalist economy." [15] He did not foresee that in a predatory capitalist economy, state intervention would be an absolute necessity to preserve human existence and to prevent the destruction of the physical environment—I speak optimistically. As Karl Polanyi, for one, has pointed out, the self-adjusting market "could not exist for any length of time without annihilating the human and natural substance of society; it would have physically destroyed man and transformed his surroundings into a wilderness."[16] Humboldt did not foresee the consequences of the commodity character of labor, the doctrine (in Polanyi's words) that "it is not for the commodity to decide where it should be offered for sale, to what purpose it should be used, at what price it should be allowed to change hands, and in what manner it should be consumed or destroyed." But the commodity, in this case, is a human life, and social protection was therefore a minimal necessity to constrain the irrational and destructive workings of the classical free market. Nor did Humboldt understand that capitalist economic relations perpetuated a form of bondage which, as early as 1767, Simon Linguet had declared to be even worse than slavery.

It is the impossibility of living by any other means that compels our farm laborers to till the soil whose fruits they will not eat, and our masons to construct buildings in which they will not live. It is want that drags them to those markets where they await masters who will do them the kindness of buying them. It is want that compels them to go down on their knees to the rich man in order to get from him permission to enrich him. . . . What effective gain has the suppression of slavery brought him? . . . He is free, you say. Ah! That is his misfortune. The slave was precious to his master because of the money he had cost him. But the handicraftsman costs nothing to the rich voluptuary who employs him. . . . These men, it is

said, have no master—they have one, and the most terrible, the
most imperious of masters, that is *need*. It is this that reduces
them to the most cruel dependence.[17]

If there is something degrading to human nature in the idea
of bondage, then a new emancipation must be awaited, Fourier's "third and last emancipatory phase of history," which will
transform the proletariat to free men by eliminating the commodity character of labor, ending wage slavery, and bringing
the commercial, industrial, and financial institutions under
democratic control.[18]

Perhaps Humboldt might have accepted these conclusions. He does agree that state intervention in social life is
legitimate if "freedom would destroy the very conditions without which not only freedom but even existence itself would be
inconceivable"—precisely the circumstances that arise in an
unconstrained capitalist economy. In any event, his criticism
of bureaucracy and the autocratic state stands as an eloquent
forewarning of some of the most dismal aspects of modern
history, and the basis of his critique is applicable to a broader
range of coercive institutions than he imagined.

Though expressing a classical liberal doctrine, Humboldt is
no primitive individualist in the style of Rousseau. Rousseau
extols the savage who "lives within himself"; he has little use
for "the sociable man, always outside of himself, [who] knows
how to live only in the opinion of others ... from [whose]
judgment alone ... he draws the sentiment of his own existence." [19] Humboldt's vision is quite different:

... the whole tenor of the ideas and arguments unfolded
in this essay might fairly be reduced to this, that while they

would break all fetters in human society, they would attempt to find as many new social bonds as possible. The isolated man is no more able to develop than the one who is fettered.

Thus he looks forward to a community of free association without coercion by the state or other authoritarian institutions, in which free men can create and inquire, and achieve the highest development of their powers—far ahead of his time, he presents an anarchist vision that is appropriate, perhaps, to the next stage of industrial society. We can perhaps look forward to a day when these various strands will be brought together within the framework of libertarian socialism, a social form that barely exists today though its elements can be perceived: in the guarantee of individual rights that has achieved its highest form—though still tragically flawed—in the Western democracies; in the Israeli *kibbutzim*; in the experiments with workers' councils in Yugoslavia; in the effort to awaken popular consciousness and create a new involvement in the social process which is a fundamental element in the Third World revolutions, coexisting uneasily with indefensible authoritarian practice.

A similar concept of human nature underlies Humboldt's work on language. Language is a process of free creation; its laws and principles are fixed, but the manner in which the principles of generation are used is free and infinitely varied. Even the interpretation and use of words involves a process of free creation. The normal use of language and the acquisition of language depend on what Humboldt calls the fixed form of language, a system of generative processes that is rooted in the nature of the human mind and constrains but does not determine the free creations of normal intelligence or, at a higher and more original level, of the great writer or thinker. Humboldt is, on the one hand, a Platonist who insists that learning is a kind of reminiscence, in which the mind, stimulated by experience, draws from its own internal resources and follows a path that it itself determines; and he is also a romantic, attuned to cultural variety, and the endless possibilities for the spiritual contributions of the creative genius. There is no contradiction in this, any more than there is a contradiction in the insistence of aesthetic theory that individual works of genius are constrained by principle and rule. The normal, creative use of language, which to the Cartesian rationalist is the best index of the existence of another mind, presupposes a system of rules and generative principles of a sort that the rationalist grammarians attempted, with some success, to determine and make explicit.

The many modern critics who sense an inconsistency in the belief that free creation takes place within—presupposes, in fact—a system of constraints and governing principles are quite mistaken; unless, of course, they speak of "contradiction" in the loose and metaphoric sense of Schelling, when he writes that "without the contradiction of necessity and freedom not only philosophy but every nobler ambition of the spirit would sink to that death which is peculiar to those sciences in which that contradiction serves no function." Without this tension between necessity and freedom, rule and choice, there can be no creativity, no communication, no meaningful acts at all.

I have discussed these traditional ideas at some length, not out of antiquarian interest, but because I think that they are valuable and essentially correct, and that they project a course we can follow with profit. Social action must be animated by a vision of a future society, and by explicit judgments of value concerning the character of this future society. These judgments must derive from some concept of the nature of man, and one may seek empirical foundations by investigating man's nature as it is revealed by his behavior and his creations, material, intellectual, and social. We have, perhaps, reached a point in history when it is possible to think seriously about a society in which freely constituted social bonds replace the fetters of autocratic institutions, rather in the sense conveyed by the remarks of Humboldt that I quoted, and elaborated more fully in the tradition of libertarian socialism in the years that followed.[20]

Predatory capitalism created a complex industrial system and an advanced technology; it permitted a considerable extension of democratic practice and fostered certain liberal values, but within limits that are now being pressed and must be overcome. It is not a fit system for the mid-twentieth century. It is incapable of meeting human needs that can be expressed only in collective terms, and its concept of competitive man who seeks only to maximize wealth and power, who subjects himself to market relationships, to exploitation and external authority, is antihuman and intolerable in the deepest sense. An autocratic state is no acceptable substitute; nor can the militarized state capitalism evolving in the United States or the bureaucratized, centralized welfare state be accepted as the goal of human existence. The only justification for repressive institutions is material and cultural deficit. But such institutions, at certain stages of history, perpetuate and produce such a deficit, and even threaten human survival. Modern science and technology can relieve men of the necessity for specialized, imbecile labor. They may, in principle, provide the basis for a rational social order based on free association and democratic control, if we have the will to create it.

A vision of a future social order is in turn based on a concept of human nature. If in fact man is an indefinitely malleable, completely plastic being, with no innate structures of mind and no intrinsic needs of a cultural or social character, then he is a fit subject for the "shaping of behavior" by the state authority, the corporate manager, the technocrat, or the central committee. Those with some confidence in the human species will hope this is not so and will try to determine the intrinsic human characteristics that provide the framework for intellectual development, the growth of moral consciousness, cultural achievement, and participation in a free community. In a partly analogous way, a classical tradition spoke of artistic genius acting within and in some ways challenging a framework of rule. Here we touch on matters that are little understood. It seems to me that we must break away, sharply and radically, from much of modern social and behavioral science if we are to move towards a deeper understanding of these matters.[21]

Here too, I think that the tradition I have briefly reviewed has a contribution to offer. As I have already observed, those who were concerned with human distinctiveness and potential repeatedly were led to a consideration of the properties of language. I think that the study of language can provide some glimmerings of understanding of rule-governed behavior and the possibilities for free and creative action within the framework of a system of rules that in part, at least, reflect intrinsic properties of human mental organization. It seems to me fair to regard the contemporary study of language as in some ways a return to the Humboldtian concept of the form of language: a system of generative processes rooted in innate properties of mind but permitting, in Humboldt's phrase, an infinite use of finite means. Language cannot be described as a system of organization of behavior. Rather, to understand how language is used, we must discover the abstract Humboldtian form of language—its generative grammar, in modern terms. To learn a language is to construct for oneself this abstract system, of course unconsciously. The linguist and psychologist can proceed to study the use and acquisition of language only insofar as he has some grasp of the properties of the system that has been mastered by the person who knows the language. Furthermore, it seems to me that a good case can be made in support of the empirical claim that such a system can be acquired, under the given conditions of time and access, only by a mind that is endowed with certain specific properties that we can now tentatively describe in some detail. As long as we restrict ourselves, conceptually, to the investigation of behavior, its organization, its development through interaction with the environment, we are bound to miss these characteristics of language and mind. Other aspects of human psychology and culture might, in principle, be studied in a similar way.

Conceivably, we might in this way develop a social science based on empirically well-founded propositions concerning human nature. Just as we study the range of humanly attainable languages, with some success, we might also try to study the forms of artistic expression or, for that matter, scientific knowledge that humans can conceive, and perhaps even the range of ethical systems and social structures in which humans can live and function, given their intrinsic capacities and needs. Perhaps one might go on to project a concept of social organization that would—under given conditions of material and spiritual culture—best encourage and accommodate the fundamental human need—if such it is—for spontaneous initiative, creative work, solidarity, pursuit of social justice.

I do not want to exaggerate, as I no doubt have, the role of investigation of language. Language is the product of human intelligence that is, for the moment, most accessible to study. A rich tradition held language to be a mirror of mind. To some extent, there is surely truth and useful insight in this idea.

I am no less puzzled by the topic "language and freedom" than when I began—and no less intrigued. In these speculative and sketchy remarks there are gaps so vast that one might question what would remain, when metaphor and unsubstantiated guess are removed. It is sobering to realize—as I believe we must—how little we have progressed in our knowledge of man and society, or even in formulating clearly the problems that might be seriously studied. But there are, I think, a few footholds that seem fairly firm. I like to believe that the intensive study of one aspect of human psychology—human language—may contribute to a humanistic social science that will serve, as well, as an instrument for social action. It must, needless to say, be stressed that social action cannot await a firmly established theory of man and society, nor can the validity of the latter be determined by our hopes and moral judgments. The two—speculation and action—must progress as best they can, looking forward to the day when theoretical inquiry will provide a firm guide to the unending, often grim, but never hopeless struggle for freedom and social justice.

NOTES

1. Notes on Anarchism

1. Octave Mirbeau, quoted in James Joll, *The Anarchists* (Boston: Little, Brown & Co., 1964), pp. 145–46.

2. Rudolf Rocker, *Anarchosyndicalism* (London: Secker & Warburg, 1938), p. 31.

3. Cited in ibid., p. 77. This quotation and that in the next sentence are from Michael Bakunin, "The Program of the Alliance," in *Bakunin on Anarchy*, ed. and trans. Sam Dolgoff (New York: Alfred A. Knopf, 1972).

4. Diego Abad de Santillán, *After the Revolution* (New York: Greenberg, 1937), p. 86. In the last chapter, written several months after the revolution had begun, he expresses his dissatisfaction with what had so far been achieved along these lines. On the accomplishments of the social revolution in Spain, see my *American Power and the New Mandarins* (New York: Pantheon Books, 1969), chap. 1, and references cited there; the important study by Broué and Témime has since been translated into English. Several other important studies have appeared since, in particular: Frank Mintz, *L'Autogestion dans l'Espagne révolutionnaire* (Paris: Editions Bélibaste, 1971); César M. Lorenzo, *Les Anarchistes espagnols et la pouvoir, 1868–1969* (Paris: Editions du Seuil, 1969); Gaston Leval, *Espagné libertaire, 1936–1939: L'Oeuvre constructive de la Révolution espagnole* (Paris: Editions du Cercle, 1971). See also Vernon Richards, *Lessons of the Spanish Revolution, 1936–1939*, enlarged edition (London: Freedom Press, 1972).

5. Cited by Robert C. Tucker, *The Marxian Revolutionary Idea* (New York: W.W. Norton & Co., 1969).

6. Bakunin, in a letter to Herzen and Ogareff, 1866. Cited by Daniel Guérin, *Jeunesse du socialism liberatire* (Paris: Librairie Marcel Rivière, 1959).

7. Fernand Pelloutier, cited in Joll, *Anarchists*. The source is "L'Anarchisme et les syndicats ouvriers," *Les Temps nouveaux*, 1895, reprinted in *Ni Dieu, ni Maître*, ed. Daniel Guerin (Lausanne: La Cité Editeur, n.d.).

8. Martin Buber, *Paths in Utopia* (Boston: Beacon Press, 1958).

9. "No state, however democratic," Bakunin wrote, "not even the reddest republic—can ever give the people what they really want, i.e., the free self-organization and administration of their own affairs from the bottom upward, without any interference or violence from above, because every state, even the pseudo–People's State concocted by Mr. Marx, is in essence only a machine ruling the masses from above, through a privileged minority of conceited intellectuals, who imagine that they know what the people need and want better than do the people themselves. . . ." "But the people will feel no better if the stick with which they are being beaten is labeled 'the people's stick' " (*Statism and Anarchy* [1873], in Dolgoff, *Bakunin on Anarchy*, p. 338)—"the people's stick" being the democratic Republic.

Marx, of course, saw the matter differently.

For discussion of the impact of the Paris Commune on this dispute, see Daniel Guérin's comments in *Ni Dieu, ni Maître*; these also appear, slightly extended, in his *Pour un marxisme libertaire* (Paris: Robert Laffont, 1969). See also note 24.

10. On Lenin's "intellectual deviation" to the left during 1917, see Robert Vincent Daniels, "The State and Revolution: A Case Study in the Genesis and Transformation of Communist Ideology," *American Slavic and East European Review* 12, no. 1 (1953).

11. Paul Mattick, *Marx and Keynes: The Limits of the Mixed Economy* (Boston: Porter Sargent, 1969), p. 295.

12. Michael Bakunin, "La Commune de Paris et la notion de l'état," reprinted in Guérin, *Ni Dieu, ni Maître*. Bakunin's final remark on the laws of individual nature as the condition of freedom can be compared with the approach to creative thought developed in the rationalist and romantic traditions, discussed in chapter 9 of my *For Reasons of State* (New York: Pantheon Books, 1973). See my *Cartesian Linguistics* (New York: Harper & Row, 1966) and *Language and Mind* (New York: Harcourt, Brace & World, 1968).

13. Shlomo Avineri, *The Social and Political Thought of Karl Marx* (London: Cambridge University Press, 1968), p. 142, referring to comments in *The Holy Family*. Avineri states that within the socialist movement only the Israeli *kibbutzim* "have perceived that the modes and forms of present social organization will determine the structure of future society." This, however, was a characteristic position of anarchosyndicalism, as noted earlier.

14. Rocker, *Anarchosyndicalism*, p. 28.

15. See Guérin's works cited earlier.

16. Karl Marx, *Critique of the Gotha Programme.*

17. Karl Marx, *Grundrisse der Kritik der Politischen Ökonomie*, cited by Mattick, *Marx and Keynes*, p. 306. In this connection, see also Mattick's essay "Workers' Control," in *The New Left*, ed. Priscilla Long (Boston: P. Sargent, 1969); and Avineri, *Social and Political Thought of Marx.*

18. Karl Marx, *Capital*, quoted by Robert Tucker, who rightly emphasizes that Marx sees the revolutionary more as a "frustrated producer" than a "dissatisfied consumer" (*Marxian Revolutionary Idea*). This more radical critique of capitalist relations of production is a direct outgrowth of the libertarian thought of the Enlightenment.

19. Marx, *Capital*, cited by Avineri, *Social and Political Thought of Marx*, p. 233.

20. Pelloutier, "L'Anarchisme."

21. "Qu'est-ce que la propriéte?" The phrase "property is theft" displeased Marx, who saw in its use a logical problem, theft presupposing the legitimate existence of property. See Avineri, *Social and Political Thought of Marx.*

22. Cited in Buber's *Paths in Utopia*, p. 19.

23. Cited in J. Hampden Jackson, *Marx, Proudhon and European Socialism* (New York: Collier Books, 1962).

24. Karl Marx, *The Civil War in France* (New York: International Publishers, 1941), p. 24. Avineri observes that this and other comments of Marx about the Commune refer pointedly to intentions and plans. As Marx made plain elsewhere, his considered assessment was more critical than in this address.

25. For some background, see Walter Kendall, *The Revolutionary Movement in Britain, 1900–1921* (London: Weidenfeld & Nicolson, 1969).

26. *Collectivisations: L'Oeuvre constructive de la Révolution espagnole*, p. 8.

27. For discussion, see Mattick, *Marx and Keynes*, and Michael Kidron, *Western Capitalism Since the War* (London: Weidenfeld & Nicolson, 1968). See also discussion and references cited in my *At War with Asia* (New York: Pantheon Books, 1970), chap. 1, pp. 23–26.

28. See Hugh Scanlon, *The Way Forward for Workers' Control*, Institute for Workers' Control Pamphlet Series, no. 1 (Nottingham, England, 1968).

29. Guérin, *Ni Dieu, ni Maître*, introduction.

30. Ibid.

31. Arthur Rosenberg, *A History of Bolshevism from Marx to the First Five Years' Plan*, trans. Ian F. Morrow (New York: Russell & Russell, 1965).

32. Marx, *Civil War in France*, pp. 62–63.

3. Part II of *Objectivity and Liberal Scholarship*

1. Cited in Paul Avrich, *The Russian Anarchists* (Princeton, NJ: Princeton University Press, 1967), pp. 93–94. A recent reformulation of this view is given by Anton Pannekoek, the Dutch scientist and spokesman for libertarian communism, in his *Workers Councils* (Melbourne, 1950), pp. 36–37:

> It is not for the first time that a ruling class tries to explain, and so to perpetuate, its rule as the consequences of an inborn difference between two kinds of people, one destined by nature to ride, the other to be ridden. The landowning aristocracy of former centuries defended their privileged position by boasting their extraction from a nobler race of conquerors that had subdued the lower race of common people. Big capitalists explain their dominating place by the assertion that they have brains and other people have none. In the same way now especially the intellectuals, considering themselves the rightful rulers of to-morrow, claim their spiritual superiority. They form the rapidly increasing class of university-trained officials and free professions, specialized in mental work, in study of books and of science, and they consider themselves as the people most gifted with intellect. Hence they are destined to be leaders of the production, whereas the ungifted mass shall execute the manual work, for which no brains are needed. They are no defenders of capitalism; not capital, but intellect should direct labor. The more so, since now society is such a complicated structure, based on abstract and difficult science, that only the highest intellectual acumen is capable of embracing, grasping and handling it. Should the working masses, from lack of insight, fail to acknowledge this need of superior intellectual lead, should they stupidly try to take the direction into their own hands, chaos and ruin will be the inevitable consequence.

2. See Daniel Bell, "Notes on the Post-Industrial Society: Part I," *Public Interest*, no. 6 (1967), pp. 24–35. Albert Parry has suggested that there are important similarities between the emergence of a scientific elite in the Soviet Union and the United States, in their growing role in decision making, citing Bell's thesis in support. See the *New York Times*, March 27, 1966, reporting on the Midwest Slavic Conference.

3. Letter to Herzen and Ogareff, 1866, cited in Daniel Guérin, *Jeunesse du socialism libertoire* (Paris: Librairie Marcel Rivière, 1959), p. 119.

4. Rosa Luxemburg, *The Russian Revolution*, trans. Bertram D. Wolfe (Ann Arbor: University of Michigan Press, 1961), p. 71.

5. Luxemburg, cited by Guérin, *Jeunesse du socialisme libertaire*, pp. 106–7.

6. Rosa Luxemberg, *Leninism or Marxism*, in *Russian Revolution*, p. 102.

7. For a very enlightening study of this matter, emphasizing domestic issues, see Michael Paul Rogin, *The Intellectuals and McCarthy: The Radical Specter* (Cambridge, MA: MIT Press, 1967).

8. Gabriel Jackson, *The Spanish Republic and the Civil War, 1931–1939* (Princeton, NJ: Princeton University Press, 1965).

9. Respectively, President of the Republic, Prime Minister from May until the Franco insurrection, and member of the conservative wing of the Popular Front selected by Azaña to try to set up a compromise government after the insurrection.

10. It is interesting that Douglas Pike's very hostile account of the National Liberation Front, cited earlier, emphasizes the popular and voluntary element in its striking organizational successes. What he describes, whether accurately or not one cannot tell, is a structure of interlocking self-help organizations, loosely coordinated and developed through persuasion rather than force—in certain respects, of a character that would have appealed to anarchist thinkers. Those who speak so freely of the "authoritarian Vietcong" may be correct, but they have presented little evidence to support their judgment. Of course, it must be understood that Pike regards the element of voluntary mass participation in self-help associations as the most dangerous and insidious feature of the NLF organizational structure.

Also relevant is the history of collectivization in China, which, as compared with the Soviet Union, shows a much higher reliance on persuasion and mutual aid than on force and terror, and appears to have been more successful. See Thomas P. Bernstein, "Leadership and Mass Mobilisation in the Soviet and Chinese Collectivization Campaigns of 1929–30 and 1955–56: A Comparison," *China Quarterly*, no. 31 (July–September 1967), pp. 1–47, for some interesting and suggestive comments and analysis.

The scale of the Chinese Revolution is so great and reports in depth are so fragmentary that it would no doubt be foolhardy to attempt a general evaluation. Still, all the reports I have been able to study suggest that insofar as real successes were achieved in the several stages of land reform, mutual aid, collectivization, and formation of communes, they were traceable in large part to the complex interaction of the Communist party cadres and the gradually evolving peasant associations, a relation which seems to stray far from the Leninist model of organization. This is particularly evident in William Hinton's magnificent study *Fanshen* (New York: Monthly Review Press, 1966), which is unparalleled, to my knowledge, as an analysis of a moment of profound revolutionary change. What seems to me particularly striking in his account of the early stages of revolution in one Chinese village is not only the extent to which party cadres submitted themselves to popular control, but also, and more significant, the ways in which exercise of control over steps of the revolutionary process was a factor in developing the consciousness and insight of those who took part in the revolution, not only from a political and social point of view, but also with respect to the human relationships that were created. It is interesting, in this connection, to note the strong populist element in early Chinese Marxism. For some very illuminating observations about this general matter, see Maurice Meisner, *Li Ta-chao and the Origins of Chinese Marxism* (Cambridge, MA: Harvard University Press, 1967).

I am not suggesting that the anarchist revolution in Spain—with its background of more than thirty years of education and struggle—is being relived in Asia, but rather that the spontaneous and voluntary elements in popular mass movements have probably been seriously misunderstood because of the instinctive antipathy towards such phenomena among intellectuals, and more recently, because of the insistence on interpreting them in terms of Cold War mythology.

11. Eric Hobsbawm, "The Spanish Background," *New Left Review*, no. 40 (November–December 1966), pp. 85–90.

12. José Peirats, *La C.N.T. en la revolución española*, 3 vols. (Toulouse: Ediciones C.N.T., 1951–52). Jackson makes one passing reference to it. Peirats has since published a general history of the period, *Los anarquistas en la crisis politica española* (Buenos Aires: Editorial Alfa-Argentina, 1964). This highly informative book should certainly be made available to an English-speaking audience.

13. An exception to the rather general failure to deal with the anarchist revolution is Hugh Thomas's "Anarchist Agrarian Collectives in the Spanish Civil War," in A *Century of Conflict, 1850–1950: Essays for A.J.P. Taylor*, ed. Martin Gilbert (New York: Atheneum Publishers, 1967), pp. 245–63. See note 60 below for some discussion. There is also much useful information in what to my mind is the best general history of the Civil War, *La Révolution et la guerre d'Espagne*, by Pierre Broué and Émile Témime (Paris: Les Éditions de Minuit, 1961). A concise and informative recent account is contained in Daniel Guérin, *L'Anarchisme* (Paris: Gallimard, 1965). In his extensive study, *The Spanish Civil War* (New York: Harper & Row, Publishers, 1961; paperback ed., 1963), Hugh Thomas barely refers to the popular revolution, and some of the major events are not mentioned at all—see, for example, note 51 below.

14. *Collectivisations: l'oeuvre constructive de la Révolution espagnole*, 2nd ed. (Toulouse: Éditions C.N.T., 1965). The first edition was published in Barcelona (Éditions C.N.T.-F.A.I., 1937). There is an excellent and sympathetic summary by the Marxist scholar Karl Korsch, "Collectivization

in Spain," in *Living Marxism* 4 (April 1939), pp. 179–82. In the same issue (pp. 170–71), the liberal-Communist reaction to the Spanish Civil War is summarized succinctly, and I believe accurately, as follows: "With their empty chatter as to the wonders of Bolshevik discipline, the geniality of Caballero, and the passions of the Pasionaria, the 'modern liberals' merely covered up their real desire for the destruction of all revolutionary possibilities in the Civil War, and their preparation for the possible war over the Spanish issue in the interest of their diverse fatherlands . . . what was truly revolutionary in the Spanish Civil War resulted from the direct actions of the workers and pauperized peasants, and not because of a specific form of labor organization nor an especially gifted leadership." I think that the record bears out this analysis, and I also think that it is this fact that accounts for the distaste for the revolutionary phase of the Civil War and its neglect in historical scholarship.

15. An illuminating eyewitness account of this period is that of Franz Borkenau, *The Spanish Cockpit* (1938; reprinted Ann Arbor: University of Michigan Press, 1963).

16. Figures from Guérin, *L'Anarchisme*, p. 154.

17. A useful account of this period is given by Felix Morrow, *Revolution and Counter-Revolution in Spain* (1938; reprinted London: New Park Publications, 1963).

18. Cited by Camillo Berneri in his "Lettre ouverte à la camarade Frederica [*sic*] Montseny," *Guerre de classes en Espagne* (Paris, 1946), a collection of items translated from his journal *Guerra di Classe*. Berneri was the outstanding anarchist intellectual in Spain. He opposed the policy of joining the government and argued for an alternative, more typically anarchist strategy to which I will return below. His own view towards joining the government was stated succinctly by a Catalan worker whom he quotes, with reference to the Republic of 1931: "It is always the old dog with a new collar." Events were to prove the accuracy of this analysis.

Berneri had been a leading spokesman of Italian anarchism. He left Italy after Mussolini's rise to power, and came to Barcelona on July 19, 1936. He formed the first Italian units for the antifascist war, according to anarchist historian Rudolf Rocker (*The Tragedy of Spain* [New York: Freie Arbeiter Stimme, 1937], p. 44). He was murdered, along with his older comrade Barbieri, during the May Days of 1937. (Arrested on May 5 by the Communist-controlled police, he was shot during the following night.) Hugh Thomas, in *The Spanish Civil War*, p. 428, suggests that "the assassins may have been Italian Communists" rather than the police. Thomas's book, which is largely devoted to military history, mentions Berneri's murder but makes no other reference to his ideas or role.

Berneri's name does not appear in Jackson's history.

19. Burnett Bolloten, *The Grand Camouflage: The Communist Conspiracy in the Spanish Civil War* (New York: Frederick A. Praeger, Inc., 1961), p. 86. This book, by a UP correspondent in Spain during the Civil War, contains a great deal of important documentary evidence bearing on the questions considered here. The attitude of the wealthy farmers of this area, most of them former supporters of the right-wing organizations that had now disappeared, is well described by the general secretary of the Peasant Federation, Julio Mateu: "Such is the sympathy for us [that is, the Communist party] in the Valencia countryside that hundreds and thousands of farmers would join our party if we were to let them. These farmers . . . love our party like a sacred thing . . . they [say] 'The Communist Party is our party.' Comrades, what emotion the peasants display when they utter these words" (cited in ibid., p. 86). There is some interesting speculation about the backgrounds for the writing of this very important book in H.R. Southworth, *Le mythe de la croisade de Franco* (Paris: Ruedo Ibérico, 1964; Spanish edition, same publisher, 1963).

The Communist headquarters in Valencia had on the wall two posters: "Respect the property of the small peasant" and "Respect the property of the small industrialist" (Borkenau, *Spanish Cockpit*, p. 117). Actually, it was the rich farmer as well who sought protection from the Communists, whom Borkenau describes as constituting the extreme right wing of the Republican forces. By early 1937, according to Borkenau, the Communist party was "to a large extent . . . the party of the military and administrative personnel, in the second place the party of the petty bourgeoisie and certain well-to-do peasant groups, in the third place the party of the employees, and only in the fourth place the party of the industrial workers" (p. 192). The party also attracted many police and army officers. The police chief in Madrid and the chief of intelligence, for example, were party members. In general, the party, which had been insignificant before the revolution, "gave the urban and rural middle classes a powerful access of life and vigour" as it defended them from the revolutionary forces (Bolloten, *Grand Camouflage*, p. 86). Gerald Brenan describes the situation as follows, in *The Spanish Labyrinth* (1943; reprinted Cambridge: Cambridge University Press, 1960), p. 325:

Unable to draw to themselves the manual workers, who remained firmly fixed in their unions, the Communists found themselves the refuge for all those who had suffered from the excesses of the Revolution or who feared where it might lead them. Well-to-do Catholic orange-growers in Valencia, peasants in Catalonia, small shopkeepers and business men, Army officers and Government officials enrolled in their ranks. . . . Thus [in Catalonia] one had a strange and novel situation: on the one side stood the huge compact proletariat of Barcelona with its long revolutionary tradition, and on the other the white-collar workers and *petite bourgeoisie* of the city, organized and armed by the Communist party against it.

Actually, the situation that Brenan describes is not as strange a one as he suggests. It is, rather, a natural consequence of Bolshevik elitism that the "Red bureaucracy" should act as a counterrevolutionary force except under the conditions where its present or future representatives are attempting to seize power for themselves, in the name of the masses whom they pretend to represent.

20. Bolloten, *Grand Camouflage*, p. 189. The legalization of revolutionary actions already undertaken and completed recalls the behavior of the "revolutionary vanguard" in the Soviet Union in 1918. Cf. Arthur Rosenberg, *A History of Bolshevism* (1932; republished in translation from the original German, New York: Russell & Russell, 1965), chap. 6. He describes how the expropriations, "accomplished as the result of spontaneous action on the part of workers and against the will of the Bolsheviks," were reluctantly legalized by Lenin months later and then placed under central party control. On the relation of the Bolsheviks to the anarchists in postrevolutionary Russia, interpreted from a pro-anarchist point of view, see Guérin, *L'Anarchisme*, pp. 96–125. See also Avrich, *Russian Anarchists*, Part II, pp. 123–254.

21. Bolloten, *Grand Camouflage*, p. 191.

22. Ibid., p. 194.

23. For some details, see Vernon Richards, *Lessons of the Spanish Revolution* (London: Freedom Press, 1953), pp. 83–88.

24. For a moving eyewitness account, see George Orwell, *Homage to Catalonia* (1938; reprinted New York: Harcourt, Brace & World, 1952, and Boston: Beacon Press, 1955; quotations in this book from Beacon Press edition). This brilliant book received little notice at the time of its first publication, no doubt because the picture Orwell drew was in sharp conflict with established liberal dogma. The attention that it has received as a cold-war document since its republication in 1952 would, I suspect, have been of little comfort to the author.

25. Cited by Rocker, *Tragedy of Spain*, p. 28.

26. See ibid. for a brief review. It was a great annoyance to Hitler that these interests were, to a large extent, protected by Franco.

27. Ibid., p. 35.

28. Brenan, *Spanish Labyrinth*, pp. 324f.

29. Borkenau, *Spanish Cockpit*, pp. 289–92. It is because of the essential accuracy of Borkenau's account that I think Hobsbawm ("Spanish Background") is quite mistaken in believing that the Communist policy "was undoubtedly the only one which could have won the Civil War." In fact, the Communist policy was bound to fail, because it was predicated on the assumption that the Western democracies would join the antifascist effort if only Spain could be preserved as, in effect, a Western colony. Once the Communist leaders saw the futility of this hope, they abandoned the struggle, which was not in their eyes an effort to win the Civil War, but only to serve the interests of Russian foreign policy. I also disagree with Hobsbawm's analysis of the anarchist revolution, cited earlier, for reasons that are implicit in this entire discussion.

30. Bolloten, *Grand Camouflage*, pp. 143–44.

31. Cited by Rosenberg, *History of Bolshevism*, pp. 168–69.

32. Bolloten, *Grand Camouflage*, p. 84.

33. Ibid., p. 85. As noted earlier, the "small farmer" included the prosperous orange growers, etc. (see note 19).

34. Brenan, *Spanish Labyrinth*, p. 321.

35. Correspondence from Companys to Prieto, 1939. While Companys, as a Catalonian with separatist impulses, would naturally be inclined to defend Catalonian achievements, he was surely not sympathetic to collectivization, despite his cooperative attitude during the period when the anarchists, with real power in their hands, permitted him to retain nominal authority. I know of no attempt to challenge the accuracy of his assessment. Morrow (*Revolution and Counter-Revolution in Spain*, p. 77) quotes the Catalonian Premier, the entrepreneur Juan Tarradellas, as defending the administration of the collectivized war industries against a Communist (PSUC) attack, which he termed the "most arbitrary falsehoods." There are many other reports commenting on the functioning of the collectivized industries by nonanarchist firsthand observers, that tend to support Companys. For example, the Swiss socialist Andres Oltmares is quoted by Rocker (*Tragedy of Spain*, p. 24) as saying that after the revolution the Catalonian workers' syndicates "in seven weeks accomplished fully as much as France did in fourteen months after the outbreak of the World War." Continuing, he says:

> In the midst of the civil war the Anarchists have proved themselves to be political organizers of the first rank. They kindled in everyone the required sense of responsibility, and knew how by eloquent appeals to keep alive the spirit of sacrifice for the general welfare of the people.
>
> As a Social Democrat I speak here with inner joy and sincere admiration of my experience in Catalonia. The anti-capitalist transformation

took place here without their having to resort to a dictatorship. The members of the syndicates are their own masters, and carry on production and the distribution of the products of labor under their own management with the advice of technical experts in whom they have confidence. The enthusiasm of the workers is so great that they scorn any personal advantage and are concerned only for the welfare of all.

Even Borkenau concludes, rather grudgingly, that industry was functioning fairly well, as far as he could see. The matter deserves a serious study.

36. Quoted in Richards, *Lessons of the Spanish Revolution*, pp. 46–47.

37. Ibid. Richards suggests that the refusal of the central government to support the Aragon front may have been motivated in part by the general policy of counterrevolution. "This front, largely manned by members of the C.N.T.-F.A.I., was considered of great strategic importance by the anarchists, having as its ultimate objective the linking of Catalonia with the Basque country and Asturias, i.e., a linking of the industrial region [of Catalonia] with an important source of raw materials." Again, it would be interesting to undertake a detailed investigation of this topic.

That the Communists withheld arms from the Aragon front seems established beyond question, and it can hardly be doubted that the motivation was political. See, for example, D.T. Cattell, *Communism and the Spanish Civil War* (1955; reprinted New York: Russell & Russell, 1965), p. 110. Cattell, who in general bends over backwards to try to justify the behavior of the central government, concludes that in this case there is little doubt that the refusal of aid was politically motivated. Brenan takes the same view, claiming that the Communists "kept the Aragon front without arms to spite the Anarchists." The Communists resorted to some of the most grotesque slanders to explain the lack of arms on the Aragon front; for example, the *Daily Worker* attributed the arms shortage to the fact that "the Trotskyist General Kopp had been carting enormous supplies of arms and ammunition across no-man's land to the fascists" (cited by Morrow, *Revolution and Counter-Revolution in Spain*, p. 145). As Morrow points out, George Kopp is a particularly bad choice as a target for such accusations. His record is well known, for example, from the account given by Orwell, who served under his command (see Orwell, *Homage to Catalonia*, pp. 209f). Orwell was also able to refute, from firsthand observation, many of the other absurdities that were appearing in the liberal press about the Aragon front, for example, the statement by Ralph Bates in the *New Republic* that the POUM troops were "playing football with the Fascists in no man's land." At that moment, as Orwell observes, "the P.O.U.M. troops were suffering heavy casualties and a number of my personal friends were killed and wounded."

38. Cited in *Living Marxism*, p. 172.

39. Bolloten, *Grand Camouflage*, p. 49, comments on the collectivization of the dairy trade in Barcelona, as follows: "The Anarchosyndicalists eliminated as unhygienic over forty pasteurizing plants, pasteurized all the milk in the remaining nine, and proceeded to displace all dealers by establishing their own dairies. Many of the retailers entered the collective, but some refused to do so: 'They asked for a much higher wage than that paid to the workers . . . , claiming that they could not manage on the one allotted to them' [*Tierra y Libertad*, August 21, 1937—the newspaper of the FAI, the anarchist activists]." His information is primarily from anarchist sources, which he uses much more extensively than any historian other than Peirats. He does not present any evaluation of these sources, which—like all others—must be used critically.

40. Morrow, *Revolution and Counter-Revolution in Spain*, p. 136.

41. Borkenau, *Spanish Cockpit*, p. 182.

42. Ibid., p. 183.

43. Ibid., p. 184. According to Borkenau, "it is doubtful whether Comorera is personally responsible for this scarcity; it might have arisen anyway, in pace with the consumption of the harvest." This speculation may or may not be correct. Like Borkenau, we can only speculate as to whether the village and workers' committees would have been able to continue to provision Barcelona, with or without central administration, had it not been for the policy of "abstract liberalism," which was of a piece with the general Communist-directed attempts to destroy the Revolutionary organizations and the structures developed in the Revolutionary period.

44. Orwell, *Homage to Catalonia*, pp. 109–11. Orwell's description of Barcelona in December (pp. 4–5), when he arrived for the first time, deserves more extensive quotation:

> It was the first time that I had ever been in a town where the working class was in the saddle. Practically every building of any size had been seized by the workers and was draped with red flags or with the red and black flag of the Anarchists; every wall was scrawled with the hammer and sickle and with the initials of the revolutionary parties; almost every church had been gutted and its images burnt. Churches here and there were being systematically demolished by gangs of workmen. Every shop and café had an inscription saying that it had been collectivized; even the bootblacks had been collectivized and their boxes painted red and black. Walters and shop-walkers looked you in the face and treated you as an equal. Servile and even ceremonial forms of speech had temporarily disappeared. Nobody

said "Señor" or "Don" or even "Usted"; everyone called everyone else "Comrade" and "Thou," and said "Salud!" instead of "Buenos dias." Tipping had been forbidden by law since the time of Primo de Rivera; almost my first experience was receiving a lecture from an hotel manager for trying to tip a lift-boy. There were no private motor cars, they had all been commandeered, and all the trams and taxis and much of the other transport were painted red and black. The revolutionary posters were everywhere, flaming from the walls in clean reds and blues that made the few remaining advertisements look like daubs of mud. Down the Ramblas, the wide central artery of the town where crowds of people streamed constantly to and fro, the loud-speakers were bellowing revolutionary songs all day and far into the night. And it was the aspect of the crowds that was the queerest thing of all. In outward appearance it was a town in which the wealthy classes had practically ceased to exist. Except for a small number of women and foreigners there were no "well-dressed" people at all. Practically everyone wore rough working-class clothes, or blue overalls or some variant of the militia uniform. All this was queer and moving. There was much in it that I did not understand, in some ways I did not even like it, but I recognized it immediately as a state of affairs worth fighting for. Also I believed that things were as they appeared, that this was really a workers' State and that the entire bourgeoisie had either fled, been killed, or voluntarily come over to the workers' side; I did not realize that great numbers of well-to-do bourgeois were simply lying low and disguising themselves as proletarians for the time being . . .

. . . waiting for that happy day when Communist power would reintroduce the old state of society and destroy popular involvement in the war.

In December 1936, however, the situation was still as described in the following remarks (p. 6):

Yet so far as one can judge the people were contented and hopeful. There was no unemployment, and the price of living was still extremely low; you saw very few conspicuously destitute people, and no beggars except the gipsies. Above all, there was a belief in the revolution and the future, a feeling of having suddenly emerged into an era of equality and freedom. Human beings were trying to behave as human beings and not as cogs in the capitalist machine. In the barbers' shops were Anarchist notices (the barbers were mostly Anarchists) solemnly explaining that barbers were no longer slaves. In

the streets were coloured posters appealing to prostitutes to stop being prostitutes. To anyone from the hard-boiled, sneering civilization
of the English-speaking races there was something rather pathetic in
the literalness with which these idealistic Spaniards took the hack-
neyed phrases of revolution. At that time revolutionary ballads of the
naïvest kind, all about proletarian brotherhood and the wickedness
of Mussolini, were being sold on the streets for a few centimes each.
I have often seen an illiterate militiaman buy one of these ballads,
laboriously spell out the words, and then, when he had got the hang
of it, begin singing it to an appropriate tune.

Recall the dates. Orwell arrived in Barcelona in late December 1936. Comorera's decree abolishing the workers' supply committees and the bread
committees was on January 7. Borkenau returned to Barcelona in mid-
January; Orwell, in April.

45. See Bolloten, *Grand Camouflage*, p. 74, citing the anarchist spokesman Juan Peiró, in September 1936. Like other anarchists and left-wing
Socialists, Peiró sharply condemns the use of force to introduce collectivization, taking the position that was expressed by most anarchists, as well
as by left-wing socialists such as Ricardo Zabalza, general secretary of the
Federation of Land Workers, who stated, on January 8, 1937: "I prefer a
small, enthusiastic collective, formed by a group of active and honest workers, to a large collective set up by force and composed of peasants without
enthusiasm, who would sabotage it until it failed. Voluntary collectivization
may seem the longer course, but the example of the small, well-managed
collective will attract the entire peasantry, who are profoundly realistic and
practical, whereas forced collectivization would end by discrediting socialized agriculture" (cited by Bolloten, *Grand Camouflage*, p. 59). However,
there seems no doubt that the precepts of the anarchist and left-socialist
spokesmen were often violated in practice.

46. Borkenau, *Spanish Cockpit*, pp. 219–20. Of this officer, Jackson says
only that he was "a dependable professional officer." After the fall of Málaga,
Lieutenant Colonel Villalba was tried for treason, for having deserted the
headquarters and abandoned his troops. Broué and Témime remark that it is
difficult to determine what justice there was in the charge.

47. Jesús Hernández and Juan Comorera, *Spain Organises for Victory:
The Policy of the Communist Party of Spain Explained* (London: Communist Party of Great Britain, n.d.), cited by Richards, *Lessons of the Spanish
Revolution*, pp. 99–100. There was no accusation that the phone service was
restricted, but only that the revolutionary workers could maintain "a close
check on the conversations that took place between the politicians." As

Richards further observes, "It is, of course, a quite different matter when the 'indiscreet ear' is that of the O.G.P.U."

48. Broué and Témime, *La Révolution et la guerre d'Espagne*, p. 266.

49. Jackson, *Spanish Republic and the Civil War*, p. 370. Thomas suggests that Sesé was probably killed accidentally (*Spanish Civil War*, p. 428).

50. The anarchist mayor of the border town of Puigcerdá had been assassinated in April, after Negrín's carabineros had taken over the border posts. That same day a prominent UGT member, Roldán Cortada, was murdered in Barcelona, it is presumed by CNT militants. This presumption is disputed by Peirats (*Los Anarquistos*: see note 12), who argues, with some evidence, that the murder may have been a Stalinist provocation. In reprisal, a CNT man was killed. Orwell, whose eyewitness account of the May Days is unforgettable, points out that "One can gauge the attitude of the foreign capitalist Press towards the Communist-Anarchist feud by the fact that Roldán's murder was given wide publicity, while the answering murder was carefully unmentioned" (*Homage to Catalonia*, p. 119). Similarly, one can gauge Jackson's attitude towards this struggle by his citation of Sesé's murder as a critical event, while the murder of Berneri goes unmentioned (cf. notes 18 and 49). Orwell remarks elsewhere that "In the English press, in particular, you would have to search for a long time before finding any favourable reference, at any period of the war, to the Spanish Anarchists. They have been systematically denigrated, and, as I know by my own experience, it is almost impossible to get anyone to print anything in their defence" (p. 159). Little has changed since.

51. According to Orwell (*Homage to Catalonia*, pp. 153–54), "A British cruiser and two British destroyers had closed in upon the harbour, and no doubt there were other warships not far away. The English newspapers gave it out that these ships were proceeding to Barcelona 'to protect British interests,' but in fact they made no move to do so; that is, they did not land any men or take off any refugees. There can be no certainty about this, but it was at least inherently likely that the British Government, which had not raised a finger to save the Spanish Government from Franco, would intervene quickly enough to save it from its own working class." This assumption may well have influenced the left-wing leadership to restrain the Barcelona workers from simply taking control of the whole city, as apparently they could easily have done in the initial stages of the May Days.

Hugh Thomas comments (*Spanish Civil War*, p. 428) that there was "no reason" for Orwell's "apprehension" on this matter. In the light of the British record with regard to Spain, it seems to me that Thomas is simply unrealistic, as compared with Orwell, in this respect.

52. Orwell, *Homage to Catalonia*, pp. 143–44.

53. *Controversy*, August 1937, cited by Morrow, *Revolution and Counter-Revolution in Spain*, p. 173. The prediction was incorrect, though not unreasonable. Had the Western powers and the Soviet Union wished, compromise would have been possible, it appears, and Spain might have been saved the terrible consequences of a Franco victory. See Brenan, *Spanish Labyrinth*, p. 331. He attributes the British failure to support an armistice and possible reconciliation to the fact that Chamberlain "saw nothing disturbing in the prospect of an Italian and German victory." It would be interesting to explore more fully the attitude of Winston Churchill. In April 1937 he stated that a Franco victory would not harm British interests. Rather, the danger was a "success of the trotskyists and anarchists" (cited by Broué and Témime, *La Révolution et la guerre d'Espagne*, p. 172). Of some interest, in this connection, is the recent discovery of an unpublished Churchill essay written in March 1939—six months after Munich—in which he said that England "would welcome and aid a genuine Hitler of peace and toleration" (see *New York Times*, December 12, 1965).

54. I find no mention at all in Hugh Thomas, *Spanish Civil War*. The account here is largely taken from Broué and Témime, *La Révolution et la guerre d'Espagne*, pp. 279–80.

55. Jackson, *Spanish Republic and the Civil War*, p. 405. A footnote comments on the "leniency" of the government to those arrested. Jackson has nothing to say about the charges against Ascaso and others, or the manner in which the old order was restored in Aragon.

To appreciate these events more fully, one should consider, by comparison, the concern for civil liberties shown by Negrín on the second, antifascist front. In an interview after the war he explained to John Whitaker (*We Cannot Escape History* [New York: Macmillan Company, 1943], pp. 116–18) why his government had been so ineffective in coping with the fifth column, even in the case of known fascist agents. Negrín explained that "we couldn't arrest a man on suspicion; we couldn't break with the rules of evidence. You can't risk arresting an innocent man because you are positive in your own mind that he is guilty. You prosecute a war, yes; but you also live with your conscience." Evidently, these scruples did not pertain when it was the rights of anarchist and socialist workers, rather than fascist agents, that were at stake.

56. Cf. Broué and Témime, *La Révolution et la guerre d'Espagne*, p. 262. Ironically, the government forces included some anarchist troops, the only ones to enter Barcelona.

57. See Bolloten, *Grand Camouflage*, p. 55, n. 1, for an extensive list of sources.

58. Broué and Témime cite the socialists Alardo Prats, Fenner Brockway, and Carlo Rosselli. Borkenau, on the other hand, suspected that the role of terror was great in collectivization. He cites very little to substantiate his feeling, though some evidence is available from anarchist sources. See note 45 above. Some general remarks on collectivization by Rosselli and Brockway are cited by Rudolf Rocker in his essay "Anarchism and Anarchosyndicalism," in n. 1, *Anarchism*, ed. Paul Eltzbacher (London, Freedom Press, 1960), p. 266:

> Rosselli: In three months Catalonia has been able to set up a new social order on the ruins of an ancient system. This is chiefly due to the Anarchists, who have revealed a quite remarkable sense of proportion, realistic understanding, and organizing ability.... All the revolutionary forces of Catalonia have united in a program of Syndicalist-Socialist character ... Anarcho-Syndicalism, hitherto so despised, has revealed itself as a great constructive force. I am no Anarchist, but I regard it as my duty to express here my opinion of the Anarchists of Catalonia, who have all too often been represented as a destructive if not a criminal element.
>
> Brockway: I was impressed by the strength of the C.N.T. It was unnecessary to tell me that it is the largest and most vital of the working class organizations in Spain. That was evident on all sides. The large industries were clearly in the main in the hands of the C.N.T.— railways, road transport, shipping, engineering, textiles, electricity, building, agriculture.... I was immensely impressed by the constructive revolutionary work which is being done by the C.N.T. Their achievements of workers' control in industry is an inspiration.... There are still some Britishers and Americans who regard the Anarchists of Spain as impossible, undisciplined uncontrollables. This is poles away from the truth. The Anarchists of Spain, through the C.N.T., are doing one of the biggest constructive jobs ever done by the working class. At the front they are fighting Fascism. Behind the front they are actually constructing the new workers' society. They see that the war against Fascism and the carrying through of the social revolution are inseparable. Those who have seen them and understood what they are doing must honor them and be grateful to them.... That is surely the biggest thing which has hitherto been done by the workers in any part of the world.

59. Cited by Richards, *Lessons of the Spanish Revolution*, pp. 76–81, where long descriptive quotations are given.

60. See Hugh Thomas, "Anarchist Agrarian Collectives in the Spanish Civil War" (note 13). He cites figures showing that agricultural production went up in Aragon and Castile, where collectivization was extensive, and down in Catalonia and the Levant, where peasant proprietors were the dominant element.

Thomas's is, to my knowledge, the only attempt by a professional historian to assess the data on agricultural collectivization in Spain in a systematic way. He concludes that the collectives were probably "a considerable social success" and must have had strong popular support, but he is more doubtful about their economic viability. His suggestion that "Communist pressure on the collectives may have given them the necessary urge to survive" seems quite unwarranted, as does his suggestion that "the very existence of the war . . . may have been responsible for some of the success the collectives had." On the contrary, their success and spontaneous creation throughout Republican Spain suggest that they answered to deeply felt popular sentiments, and both the war and Communist pressure appear to have been highly disruptive factors—ultimately, of course, destructive factors.

Other dubious conclusions are that "in respect of redistribution of wealth, anarchist collectives were hardly much improvement over capitalism" since "no effective way of limiting consumption in richer collectives was devised to help poorer ones," and that there was no possibility of developing large-scale planning. On the contrary, Bolloten (*Grand Camouflage*, pp. 176–79) points out that "In order to remedy the defects of collectivization, as well as to iron out discrepancies in the living standards of the workers in flourishing and impoverished enterprises, the Anarchosyndicalists, although rootedly opposed to nationalization, advocated the centralization—or, socialization, as they called it—under trade union control, of entire branches of production." He mentions a number of examples of partial socialization that had some success, citing as the major difficulty that prevented still greater progress the insistence of the Communist party and the UGT leadership—though apparently not all of the rank-and-file members of the UGT—on government ownership and control. According to Richards (*Lessons of the Spanish Revolution*, p. 82): "In June, 1937 . . . a National Plenum of Regional Federations of Peasants was held in Valencia to discuss the formation of a National Federation of Peasants for the coordination and extension of the collectivist movement and also to ensure an equitable distribution of the produce of the land, not only between the collectives but for the whole country. Again in Castille in October 1937, a merging of the 100,000 members of the Regional Federation of Peasants and the 13,000 members in the food distributive trades took place. It represented a logical step in ensuring better co-ordination, and was accepted for the whole of Spain at the National Congress of Collectives held in Valencia in November 1937." Still other plans were under consideration for regional and national coordination—see, for example, D.A. de Santillán, *After the Revolution* (New York: Greenberg, 1937), for some ideas.

Thomas feels that collectives could not have survived more than "a few years while primitive misery was being overcome." I see nothing in his data to support this conclusion. The Palestinian experience has shown that collectives can remain both a social and an economic success over a long period. The success of Spanish collectivization, under war conditions, seems amazing. One can obviously not be certain whether these successes could have been secured and extended had it not been for the combined fascist, Communist, and liberal attack, but I can find no objective basis for the almost universal skepticism. Again, this seems to me merely a matter of irrational prejudice.

61. The following is a brief description by the anarchist writer Gaston Leval, *Né Franco, Né Stalin, le collettività anarchiche spagnole nella lotta contro Franco e la reazione staliniana* (Milan: Istituto Editoriale Italiano, 1952), pp. 303f; sections reprinted in *Collectivités anarchistes en Espagne révolutionnaire, Noir et Rouge*, undated.

> In the middle of the month of June, the attack began in Aragon on a grand scale and with hitherto unknown methods. The harvest was approaching. Rifles in hand, treasury guards under Communist orders stopped trucks loaded with provisions on the highways and brought them to their offices. A little later, the same guards poured into the collectives and confiscated great quantities of wheat under the authority of the general staff with headquarters in Barbastro. . . . Later open attacks began, under the command of Lister with troops withdrawn from the front at Belchite more than 50 kilometers away, in the month of August. . . . The final result was that 30 percent of the collectives were completely destroyed. In Alcolea, the municipal council that governed the collective was arrested; the people who lived in the Home for the Aged . . . were thrown out on the street. In Mas de las Matas, in Monzon, in Barbastro, on all sides, there were arrests. Plundering took place everywhere. The stores of the cooperatives and their grain supplies were rifled; furnishings were destroyed. The governor of Aragon, who was appointed by the central government after the dissolution of the Council of Aragon—which appears to have been the signal for the armed attack against the collectives— protested. He was told to go to the devil.
>
> On October 22, at the National Congress of Peasants, the

delegation of the Regional Committee of Aragon presented a report of which the following is the summary:

"More than 600 organizers of collectives have been arrested. The government has appointed management committees that seized the warehouses and distributed their contents at random. Land, draught animals, and tools were given to individual families or to the fascists who had been spared by the revolution. The harvest was distributed in the same way. The animals raised by the collectives suffered the same fate. A great number of collectivized pig farms, stables, and dairies were destroyed. In certain communes, such as Bordon and Calaceite, even seed was confiscated and the peasants are now unable to work the land."

The estimate that 30 percent of the collectives were destroyed is consistent with figures reported by Peirats (*Los anarquistas en la crisis política española*, p. 300). He points out that only 200 delegates attended the congress of collectives of Aragon in September 1937 ("held under the shadow of the bayonets of the Eleventh Division" of Lister) as compared with 500 delegates at the congress of the preceding February. Peirats states that an army division of Catalan separatists and another division of the PSUC also occupied parts of Aragon during this operation, while three anarchist divisions remained at the front, under orders from the CNT-FAI leadership. Compare Jackson's explanation of the occupation of Aragon: "The peasants were known to hate the Consejo, *the anarchists had deserted the front during the Barcelona fighting*, and the very existence of the Consejo was a standing challenge to the authority of the central government" (italics mine).

62. Regarding Bolloten's work, Jackson has this to say: "Throughout the present chapter, I have drawn heavily on this carefully documented study of the Communist Party in 1936–37. It is unrivaled in its coverage of the wartime press, of which Bolloten, himself a UP correspondent in Spain, made a large collection" (p. 363, n. 4).

63. See note 18. A number of citations from Berneri's writings are given by Broué and Témime. Morrow also presents several passages from his journal, *Guerra di Classe*. A collection of his works would be a very useful contribution to our understanding of the Spanish Civil War and to the problems of revolutionary war in general.

64. Cattell, *Communism and the Spanish Civil War*, p. 208. See also the remarks by Borkenau, Brenan, and Bolloten cited earlier. Neither Cattell nor Borkenau regards this decline of fighting spirit as a major factor, however.

65. Broué and Témime, *La Révolution et la guerre d'Espagne*, p. 195, n. 7.

66. To this extent, Trotsky took a similar position. See his *Lesson of Spain* (London: Workers' International Press, 1937).

67. Cited in Richards, *Lessons of the Spanish Revolution*, p. 23.

68. H.E. Kaminski, *Ceux de Barcelone* (Paris: Les Éditions Denoël, 1937), p. 181. This book contains very interesting observations on anarchist Spain by a skeptical though sympathetic eyewitness.

69. May 15, 1937. Cited by Richards, *Lessons of the Spanish Revolution*, p. 106.

70. Cited by Broué and Témime, *La Révolution et la guerre d'Espagne*, p. 258, n. 34. The conquest of Saragossa was the goal, never realized, of the anarchist militia in Aragon.

71. Ibid., p. 175.

72. Ibid., p. 193.

73. The fact was not lost on foreign journalists. Morrow (*Revolution and Counter-Revolution in Spain*, p. 68) quotes James Minifie in the *New York Herald Tribune*, April 28, 1937: "A reliable police force is being built up quietly but surely. The Valencia government discovered an ideal instrument for this purpose in the Carabineros. These were formerly customs officers and guards, and always had a good reputation for loyalty. It is reported on good authority that 40,000 have been recruited for this force, and that 20,000 have already been armed and equipped. . . . The anarchists have already noticed and complained about the increased strength of this force at a time when we all know there's little enough traffic coming over the frontiers, land or sea. They realize that it will be used against them." Consider what these soldiers, as well as Lister's division or the *asaltos* described by Orwell, might have accomplished on the Aragon front, for example. Consider also the effect on the militiamen, deprived of arms by the central government, of the knowledge that these well-armed, highly trained troops were liquidating the accomplishments of their revolution.

74. Cited in Rocker, *Tragedy of Spain*, p. 37.

75. For references, see Bolloten, *Grand Camouflage*, p. 192, n. 12.

76. Cited in Rocker, *Tragedy of Spain*, p. 37.

77. Liston M. Oak, "Balance Sheet of the Spanish Revolution," *Socialist Review* 6 (September 1937), pp. 7–9, 26. This reference was brought to my attention by William B. Watson. A striking example of the distortion introduced by the propaganda efforts of the 1930s is the strange story of the influential film *The Spanish Earth*, filmed in 1937 by Joris Ivens with a text (written afterwards) by Hemingway—a project that was apparently intitiated by Dos Passos. A very revealing account of this matter, and of the perception of the Civil War by Hemingway and Dos Passos, is given in W.B. Watson and Barton Whaley, "The Spanish Earth of Dos Passos and Hemingway,"

unpublished, 1967. The film dealt with the collectivized village of Fuenti-dueña in Valencia (a village collectivized by the UGT, incidentally). For the libertarian Dos Passos, the revolution was the dominant theme; it was the antifascist war, however, that was to preoccupy Hemingway. The role of Dos Passos was quickly forgotten, because of the fact (as Watson and Whaley point out) that "Dos Passos had become anathema to the Left for his criticisms of communist policies in Spain."

78. As far as the East is concerned, Rocker (*Tragedy of Spain*, p. 25) claims that "the Russian press, for reasons that are easily understood, never uttered one least little word about the efforts of the Spanish workers and peasants at social reconstruction." I cannot check the accuracy of this claim, but it would hardly be surprising if it were correct.

79. See Patricia A.M. Van der Esch, *Prelude to War: The International Repercussions of the Spanish Civil War (1935–1939)* (The Hague: Martinus Nijhoff, 1951), p. 47, and Brenan, *Spanish Labyrinth*, p. 329, n. 1. The conservative character of the Basque government was also, apparently, largely a result of French pressure. See Broué and Témime, *La Révolution et la guerre d'Espagne*, p. 172, n. 8.

80. See Dante A. Puzzo, *Spain and the Great Powers: 1936–1941* (New York: Columbia University Press, 1962), pp. 86f. This book gives a detailed and very insightful analysis of the international background of the Civil War.

81. Jules Sauerwein, dispatch to the *New York Times* dated July 26. Cited by Puzzo, *Spain and the Great Powers*, p. 84.

82. Cf., for example, Jackson, *Spanish Republic and the Civil War*, pp. 248f.

83. As reported by Herschel V. Johnson of the American embassy in London; cited by Puzzo, *Spain and the Great Powers*, p. 100.

84. See Broué and Témime, *La Révolution et la guerre d'Espagne*, pp. 288–89.

85. Cited by Thomas, *Spanish Civil War*, p. 531, n. 3. Rocker, *Tragedy of Spain*, p. 14, quotes (without reference) a proposal by Churchill for a five-year "neutral dictatorship" to "tranquilize" the country, after which they could "perhaps look for a revival of parliamentary institutions."

86. Puzzo, *Spain and the Great Powers*, p. 116.

87. Ibid., p. 147. Eden is referring, of course, to the Soviet Union. For an analysis of Russian assistance to the Spanish Republic, see Cattell, *Communism and the Spanish Civil War*, chap. 8.

88. Cf. Puzzo, *Spain and the Great Powers*, pp. 147–48.

89. Ibid., p. 212.

90. Ibid., p. 93.

91. Jackson, *Spanish Republic and the Civil War*, p. 248.

92. Puzzo, *Spain and the Great Powers*, pp. 151f.

93. Ibid., pp. 154–55 and n. 27.

94. For some references, see Allen Guttmann, *The Wound in the Heart: America and the Spanish Civil War* (New York: The Free Press, 1962), pp. 137–38. The earliest quasi-official reference that I know of is in Herbert Feis, *The Spanish Story* (New York: Alfred A. Knopf, 1948), where data is given in an appendix. Jackson (*Spanish Republic and the Civil War*, p. 256) refers to this matter, without noting that Texaco was violating a prior agreement with the Republic. He states that the American government could do nothing about this, since "oil was not considered a war material under the Neutrality Act." He does not point out, however, that Robert Cuse, the Martin Company, and the Mexican government were put under heavy pressure to withhold supplies from the Republic, although this too was quite legal. As noted, the Texaco Company was never even branded "unethical" or "unpatriotic," these epithets of Roosevelt's being reserved for those who tried to assist the Republic. The cynic might ask just why oil was excluded from the Neutrality Act of January 1937, noting that while Germany and Italy were capable of supplying arms to Franco, they could not meet his demands for oil.

The Texaco Oil Company continued to act upon the pro-Nazi sympathies of its head, Captain Thorkild Rieber, until August 1940, when the publicity began to be a threat to business. See Feis, *Spanish Story*, for further details. For more on these matters, see Richard P. Traina, *American Diplomacy and the Spanish Civil War* (Bloomington: Indiana University Press, 1968), pp. 166f.

95. Puzzo, *Spain and the Great Powers*, p. 160. He remarks: "A government in Madrid in which Socialists, Communists, and anarchists sat was not without menace to American business interests both in Spain and Latin America" (p. 165). Hull, incidentally, was in error about the acts of the Spanish government. The irresponsible left-wing elements had not been given arms but had seized them, thus preventing an immediate Franco victory.

96. See Jackson, *Spanish Republic and the Civil War*, p. 458.

97. Cf. Guttmann, *Wound in the Heart*, p. 197. Of course, American liberalism was always pro-loyalist, and opposed both to Franco and to the revolution. The attitude towards the latter is indicated with accuracy by this comparison, noted by Guttmann, p. 165: "300 people met in Union Square to hear Liston Oak [see note 77] expose the Stalinists' role in Spain; 20,000 met in Madison Square Garden to help Earl Browder and Norman Thomas celebrate the preservation of bourgeois democracy," in July 1937.

98. Ibid., p. 198.

99. To conclude these observations about the international reaction, it should be noted that the Vatican recognized the Franco government *de facto* in August 1937 and *de jure* in May 1938. Immediately upon Franco's final victory, Pope Pius XII made the following statement: "Peace and victory have been willed by God to Spain . . . which has now given to proselytes of the materialistic atheism of our age the highest proof that above all things stands the eternal value of religion and of the Spirit." Of course, the position of the Catholic Church has since undergone important shifts—something that cannot be said of the American government.

100. See note 14.

5. Language and Freedom

1. F.W.J. Schelling, *Philosophical Inquiries into the Nature of Human Freedom*, trans. and ed. James Gutmann (Chicago: Open Court Publishing Co., 1936).

2. R.D. Masters, introduction to his edition of *First and Second Discourses*, by Jean-Jacques Rousseau (New York: St. Martin's Press, 1964).

3. Compare Proudhon, a century later: "No long discussion is necessary to demonstrate that the power of denying a man his thought, his will, his personality, is a power of life and death, and that to make a man a slave is to assassinate him."

4. Cited in Michael Bakunin, *Etatisme et anarchie*, ed. Arthur Lehning (Leiden: E.J. Brill, 1967), editor's note 50, from P. Schrecker, "Kant et la revolution française," *Revue philosophique*, September–December 1939.

5. I have discussed this matter in *Cartesian Linguistics* (New York: Harper & Row, 1966) and *Language and Mind* (New York: Harcourt, Brace & World, 1968).

6. See the references of note 5 and also my *Aspects of the Theory of Syntax* (1965; Cambridge, MA: MIT Press, 1969), chap. 1, sec. 8.

7. I need hardly add that this is not the prevailing view. For discussion, see Eric H. Lenneberg, *Biological Foundations of Language* (New York: John Wiley & Sons, 1967); my *Language and Mind*; E.A. Drewe, G. Ettlinger, A.D. Milner, and R.E. Passingham, "A Comparative Review of the Results of Behavioral Research on Man and Monkey," Institute of Psychiatry, London, unpublished draft, 1969; P.H. Lieberman, D.H. Klatt, and W.H. Wilson, "Vocal Tract Limitations on the Vowel Repertoires of Rhesus Monkey and Other Nonhuman Primates," *Science*, June 6, 1969; and P.H. Lieberman, "Primate Vocalizations and Human Linguistic Ability," *Journal of the Acoustical Society of America* 44, no. 6 (1968).

8. In the books cited above and in my *Current Issues in Linguistic Theory* (New York: Humanities Press, 1964).

9. J.W. Burrow, introduction to his edition of *The Limits of State Action*, by Wilhelm von Humboldt (London: Cambridge University Press, 1969), from which most of the following quotes are taken.

10. Compare the remarks of Kant, quoted above. Kant's essay appeared in 1793; Humboldt's was written in 1791–1792. Parts appeared but it did not appear in full during his lifetime. See Burrow, introduction to Humboldt, *Limits of State Action*.

11. Thomas G. Sanders, "The Church in Latin America," *Foreign Affairs* 48, no. 2 (1970).

12. Ibid. The source is said to be the ideas of Paulo Freire. Similar criticism is widespread in the student movement in the West. See, for example, Mitchell Cohen and Dennis Hale, eds., *The New Student Left*, rev. ed. (Boston: Beacon Press, 1967), chap. 3.

13. Namely, that a man "only attains the most matured and graceful consummation of his activity, when his way of life is harmoniously in keeping with his character"—that is, when his actions flow from inner impulse.

14. The latter quote is from Humboldt's comments on the French Constitution, 1791—parts translated in *Humanist Without Portfolio: An Anthology*, trans. and ed. Marianne Cowan (Detroit: Wayne State University Press, 1963).

15. Rudolf Rocker, "Anarchism and Anarcho-syndicalism," in Paul Eltzbacher, *Anarchism: Exponents of the Anarchist Philosophy* (London: Freedom Press, 1960). In his book *Nationalism and Culture* (London: Freedom Press, 1937), Rocker describes Humboldt as "the most prominent representative in Germany" of the doctrine of natural rights and the opposition to the authoritarian state. Rousseau he regards as a precursor of authoritarian doctrine, but he considers only the *Social Contract*, not the far more libertarian *Discourse on Inequality*. Burrow observes that Humboldt's essay anticipates "much nineteenth century political theory of a populist, anarchist and syndicalist kind" and notes the hints of the early Marx. See also my *Cartesian Linguistics*, n. 51, for some comments.

16. Karl Polanyi, *The Great Transformation: The Political and Economic Origins of Our Time* (Boston: Beacon Press, 1957).

17. Cited by Paul Mattick, "Workers' Control," in *The New Left*, ed. Priscilla Long (Boston: P. Sargent, 1969), p. 377. See also my *For Reasons of State* (New York: Pantheon Books, 1973), chap. 8.

18. Cited in Martin Buber, *Paths in Utopia* (Boston: Beacon Press, 1958).

19. Yet Rousseau dedicates himself, as a man who has lost his "original simplicity" and can no longer "do without laws and chiefs," to respect the sacred bonds" of his society and "scrupulously obey the laws, and the men who are their authors and ministers," while scorning "a constitution that can be maintained only with the help of so many respectable people . . . and from which, despite all their care, always arise more real calamities than apparent advantages."

20. See my *For Reasons of State*, chap. 8.

21. See ibid., chap. 7, for a discussion of the fraudulent claims in this regard of certain varieties of behavioral science.

PERMISSIONS

by Noam Chomsky. Published by Vintage Books. Reprinted by permission of The Random House Group Limited.

Chapter 3 first appeared in *American Power and the New Mandarins* (New York: Pantheon Books, 1969; New York: The New Press, 2003). It was reprinted in *Objectivity and Liberal Scholarship* (New York: The New Press, 2003). © 1967, 1969, 2003 by Noam Chomsky. Permission courtesy of The New Press. The excerpts from *Homage to Catalonia* by George Orwell, on pages 77–78, are reprinted by permission of Harcourt, Brace & World, Inc. Copyright © 1952 by Sonia Brownell Orwell.

Chapter 4 first appeared in Harry Kreisler's *Political Awakenings: Conversations with History* (New York: The New Press, 2010). Copyright © 2002 by Noam Chomsky. Permission courtesy of The New Press.

Chapter 5 was presented as a lecture at the University Freedom and Human Sciences Symposium, Loyola University, Chicago, January 8–9, 1970; it appeared in the Proceedings of the Symposium, edited by Thomas R. Gorman. It also was published in *Abraxas* 1, no. 1 (1970), and in *TriQuarterly*, nos. 23–24 (1972). It was reprinted in *For Reasons of State* (New York: Pantheon Books, 1973; New York: The New Press, 2003). © 1973, 2003 by Noam Chomsky. Permission courtesy of The New Press.

Noam Chomsky

WHO RULES THE WORLD?

'As long as the general population is passive, apathetic, diverted to consumerism or hatred of the vulnerable, the powerful can do as they please and those who survive will be left to contemplate the outcome.'

In the post-9/11 era, America's policy-makers have increasingly prioritised the pursuit of power, both military and economic, above all else – human rights, democracy, even security. Drawing on examples ranging from expanding drone assassination programs to civil war in Syria to the continued violence in Iraq, Iran, Afghanistan, Israel and Palestine, Noam Chomsky examines the workings of imperial power across our increasingly chaotic planet.

'The world's greatest public intellectual' *Observer*

'One of the greatest, most radical public thinkers of our time. When the sun sets on the American empire, Chomsky's work will survive' Arundhati Roy

'[Chomsky is] the closest thing in the English-speaking world to an intellectual superstar' *Guardian*

NOAM CHOMSKY

OCCUPY

Since its appearance in Zuccotti Park, New York, in September 2011, the Occupy movement has spread to hundreds of towns and cities across the world. No longer occupying small tent camps, the movement now occupies the global conscience as its messages spread from street protests to op-ed pages to the highest seats of power. From the movement's onset, Noam Chomsky has supported its critique of corporate corruption and encouraged its efforts to increase civic participation, economic equality, democracy and freedom.

Through talks and conversations with movement supporters, *Occupy* presents Chomsky's latest thinking on the central issues, questions and demands that are driving ordinary people to protest. How did we get to this point? How are the wealthiest 1% influencing the lives of the other 99%? How can we separate money from politics? What would a genuinely democratic election look like? How can we redefine basic concepts like 'growth' to increase equality and quality of life for all?

'Noam Chomsky is an inspiration all over the world – to millions, I suspect – for the simple reason that he is a truth-teller on an epic scale'
John Pilger

NOAM CHOMSKY

MAKING THE FUTURE

'The fate of democracy is at stake in Madison, Wisconsin, no less than it is in Tahrir Square.'

Making the Future is a collection of essays from Noam Chomsky, one of our most vital and provocative voices of political dissent.

Taking up the thread from 2007's *Interventions*, these penetrating and compelling articles examine numerous topics, including the financial crisis, Obama's presidency, WikiLeaks and the on-going conflicts in the Middle East.

Restating and refining his commitment to democracy and finding inspiration in the popular uprisings of the Arab Spring, *Making the Future* is Chomsky's fiercely argued and timely comment on a fast-changing world.

'Chomsky is one of a small band of individuals fighting a whole industry. And that makes him not only brilliant, but heroic'
Arundhati Roy

NOAM CHOMSKY

POWER SYSTEMS

In this collection of conversations, conducted from 2010 to 2012, Noam Chomsky explores the most immediate and urgent concerns: the future of democracy in the Arab world, the implications of the Fukushima nuclear disaster, the 'class war' fought by U.S. business interests against working people and the poor, the breakdown of mainstream political institutions and the rise of the far right.

These interviews, conducted with David Barsamian, will inspire a new generation of readers and longtime Chomsky fans eager to understand the many crises we now confront, both at home and abroad.

'Noam Chomsky is a global phenomenon . . . he may be the most widely read American voice on foreign policy on the planet to-day' *New York Times Book Review*